Let's Go Fishing

Written by Deana Carmack

Published by Graph Publishing, LLC
110 N. Seaman St.
Eastland, Texas 76448

Copyright © Deana Carmack, 2019
All rights reserved
Front Cover photo: Geoffrey Whiteway
Back Cover photo: Geoffrey Whiteway
Graphics by: Deana Carmack, Joe Schiller
Photos by: Chance Agrella, Universe Today, Beverly O'Malley
Illustrations by: Wikipedia Commons, pbs.org, Clipart wiki, Science photo library, Answers in Genesis, Free Bible images, Hiveminer, Baptist Tabernacle, Crisis Magazine, Cagnz, Biblical Foundations, Church of Jesus Christ

Bible Scripture references:
King James Version
New International Version: Zondervan Bible Publishers
Creation poem by Deana Carmack © 2019

ISBN 978-1-7329755-6-9

Printed in the United States of America
Set in Calibri font
Designed and formatted by Deana Carmack

With the exception of the pages in this book for which copying by the teachers who purchase and use this curriculum is permitted, no part of this publication may be reproduced, stored in or introduced into a retrieval system, or transmitted, in any form or by any means (electronic, mechanical, photocopying, recording or otherwise), without the prior written permission of both the copyright owner and the above publisher of this book.

The scanning, uploading, and distribution of this book or any portion of it via the Internet or via any other means without the permission of the publisher is illegal and punishable by law. Please purchase only authorized electronic editions and do not participate in or encourage electronic piracy of copyrightable materials. Your support of the author's rights is appreciated.

Library of Congress Cataloguing-in-Publication Data

Let's Go Fishing children's Bible curriculum: thirteen lessons beginning with Genesis 1
ISBN 978-1-7329755-6-9
1. Christian Education, childhood and youth—Old Testament

Please read

Hello, fellow teachers: I'm assuming, since you are involved in children's ministry, that your heart is devoted to God and to the children you teach. This series of lessons has been a goal of mine for many, many years. A number of teachers have voiced their concern and frustration that there didn't seem to be available a children's curriculum that had any "meat" to it.

This curriculum is an earnest effort to address that lack and to provide a study that the kids can "get into" and the teachers can enjoy presenting. If you believe, as I do, that reaching children for Christ at an early, or even not-so-early, age is absolutely vital to ensuring their place in the Kingdom, then we hope you'll scan through the pages of this text and discover that it deals with who God is, how much He loves us, and why He should be #1 in our lives.

Each lesson comes complete with strategies and concepts that have been developed and proven successful over a virtual lifetime of teaching children. It includes ideas for music, scripture memory, and methods of presentation that we hope you'll find easy to understand and follow. The detailed teaching ideas are designed to aid in presenting the lessons and are in no way intended to cramp your individual teaching styles and imagination. In other words, "Go For It!"

We've placed the music segment of the lessons near the beginning of each presentation because experience has taught us that singing is one of the surest ways to get the kids engaged in the lesson. They'll remember the music long after they've forgotten the text. (But don't worry about that. The Spirit will insure that the seeds we've planted will take root and sprout when the time is right.) The music suggestions are offered to complement the lessons and may be garnered from a number of sources. If your class has a "smart" TV or a computer or tablet with wifi connections, you may find all, or nearly all, of the songs on YouTube.

Since most of us have experienced the unreliability of the internet on more than one occasion, we encourage you to have a "plan B". Other sources can include hymnals, CD's or DVD's. (Please see the next page for a list of items that will be helpful in presenting your lessons.)These are not included with the curriculum because you may already have some or all of them, but may be purchased from Christian supply companies, (Mardel's, Christian Book Distributors, etc.) or individually from Amazon or ebay, etc.

I recommend the purchase of *"100 Singalong Bible Songs for Kids"* (CD or DVD) by Cedarmont Kids, *Bible Singalong Collections* by Cedarmont, and the *PraiseBaby* collection by Big House Kids because these collections contain so many songs that children really enjoy. The PraiseBaby collection contains songs of praise and, despite its name, is really a compilation of praise songs that are suitable for any age.

We also encourage the children to learn to use their Bibles. If your students are able to read, we often suggest that the children, themselves, read the scripture passages. As I'm sure you know, the Word of God has a power to change hearts and lives like nothing else can.

I choose the New International Version for most Scripture references, but occasionally, the King James Version is quoted for memory verses because that's the one most of us are familiar with. Whichever version you prefer is fine so long as it is an accurate translation and not just a paraphrased version of the Scripture. We are directed to be familiar with the Scripture and discerning in its use.

This series of lessons begins, of course, at the beginning...of time, of creation, and of God's revelation of Himself to mankind. The lessons continue through the Bible, most often using the accounts of mere mortals, like ourselves, to demonstrate the attributes of God.

I'm not sure it's possible to include everything that's valuable in any curriculum, so please feel free, in fact we encourage you, to add visuals or activities to your class that will make these lessons more colorful, helpful and appealing. I suggest that you make copies of the memory verses on cardstock, brown packaging paper, etc. and tack or tape them to the walls in your room. You can make games of memory verses by saying the first part of the verse and having the students complete it. Hiding His Word in our hearts is vital when it comes to the daily struggle to "hold the line" against the temptations of Satan, and, sometimes, even our culture.

Matthew 4:19 records these words… "Come, follow me," Jesus said, "and I will make you fishers of men."

We're fishing for and fighting (yes, we are in a battle) for the hearts and souls of the precious children God has placed in our pathways.

So, come on! Let's go fishing!

LET'S GO FISHING! TABLE OF CONTENTS

1. Audio-visual Resources…………5

2. Music Selections……………..6

3. Lesson 1, God, the Spirit…………7

4. Lesson 2, The Creation, Days 1-3………..18

5. Lesson 3, The Creation, Days 4 & 5………..32

6. Lesson 4, The Creation, Day 6…Animals………..46

7. Lesson 5, Roundup, Review & Introduction to the Bible………..60

8. Lesson 6, The Creation of Man and the Triune God………..66

9. Lesson 7, The Creation of Adam………..75

10. Lesson 8, The Creation of Eve and the Fall of Man………..85

11. Lesson 9, Adam and Eve Expelled from the Garden………..94

12. Lesson 10, Lesson Review and Bible Games………..102

13. Lesson 11, Noah, Part 1………..109

14. Lesson 12, Noah and His Family Return to the Land………..122

15. Lesson 13, God Calls Abram………..133

16. List of Memory Verses………..146

AUDIO/VISUAL RESOURCES

1. Cedarmont Kids DVD/CD's
2. Maranatha CD's
3. Group Lifetree
4. Young Praise
5. YouTube
6. Intellectual Baby Music Video
7. Lifetree Kids
8. PraiseBaby

Videos:
YouTube: *God's Creation According to Genesis* (Praiseshark)
       Creation (Saddleback Kids)
DVD: *Animated Bible Stories, The Creation*

LET'S GO FISHING! BIBLE CURRICULUM: MUSIC SELECTIONS

Songs that Praise God
- My God is So big…Cedarmont Kids
- Hallelu, Hallelu, Hallelu, Hallelujah! 50 songs of Praise, Cedarmont Kids
- He's Got the Whole World in His Hands…Lifetree kids
- I'm Gonna Sing, Sing, Sing…Cedarmont Kids (Bible Singalong Collection 2)
- What a Mighty God We Serve…Cedarmont Kids
- God Can Do Anything…Young Praise, YouTube
- How Great Is Our God…PraiseBaby Collection (My Father's World CD)
- Shout to the Lord…Praise Baby Collection (Praises and Smiles CD)
- God Can Do Anything but Fail
- Great Is the Lord…PraiseBaby Collection (God of Wonders CD)
- Lord of All Creation
- The Fruit of the Spirit's Not a Coconut
- I Love You, Lord
- The Boss of Me Crossroad Kids Club
- Creation Song…Saddleback Kids
- I'm Gonna Sing, Sing, Sing…Cedarmont Kids CD
- He Is Lord…Cedarmont Kids CD
- Rise and Shine
- Alive, Alive
- This is My Commandment
- Father Abraham
- Who Built the Ark?
- Isn't He Wonderful?

- I Have Decided to Follow Jesus
- Wide, Wide as the Ocean

LET'S GO FISHING, LESSON 1
GOD, the Father, GOD, the Son, and GOD, the Holy Spirit

For your spirit:

> "Know therefore that the Lord, your God, is GOD; he is the faithful God, keeping his covenant of love to a thousand generations of those who love him and keep his commands." Deuteronomy 7:9.
>
> "God said to Moses, I AM who I AM." Exodus 3:14...
>
> "Taste and see that the Lord is good; blest is he who takes refuge in him." Psalm 34:8
>
> "...one Lord, one faith, one baptism; one God and Father of all, who is over all and through all and in all." Ephesians 4:5, 6

Scripture reference: John 4:23, 24

Memory verse:
    "**God is spirit, and his worshipers must worship in spirit and in truth**." John 4:24

Supplies needed:

- A Bible for each child (I like to use "same edition" copies of the same version in order to make it easier for the students to locate verses.)
- Music DVD (Hillsong) or CD (or YouTube)..."What a Mighty God We Serve" and/or "My God is So Big" (Cedarmont Kids CD or DVD)
- (**option 1**) Two balloons, one flat, the other inflated
- Optional: a balloon for each student
- (**option 2**) A drinking straw and a plastic bead for each student
- A copy of figure 1
- A copy of figure 2
- Enough copies of figure 3 for each child to have one to take home to his/her parents (There are 7 individual notes per sheet.)

- Optional: a dry-erase board and dry-erase markers

- Snacks (optional) and whatever supplies you need to go with them...cups, napkins or saucers, ice, drinks, etc. Please make an effort to keep the sugar content of your snacks down to a minimum...fruit, crackers, cheese crackers, snack bars, etc. fill the bill.
- (If your students are not acquainted with the "Lord's Prayer," it helps to have it printed on a dry-erase board or other visual.)

Teacher prep:
1. Pray for each child
2. Pray for yourself and any assistants you may have in your class.
3. Be prepared....know your lesson and its emphasis well so you can tell it with only occasional glances at your notes. Also be familiar with the songs.
4. Snacks (optional)...many classes like to offer snacks during the Sunday School session. I've found that it usually works better if snack time is saved for the end of class. Offering them at the beginning of class often makes it more difficult to move into the lesson.

Welcome: Greet each child as he/she enters the room. While waiting for others or after all are seated, ask questions about the week just past.

- ❖ The lure

Music "What a Mighty God We Serve" and/or "My God Is So Big" (Children often like to stand while singing...it makes it easier to add actions.)

Invite the children to be seated.

We like to begin every session with the Lord's Prayer or a personal prayer. (It doesn't matter too much which version of the Bible you prefer. We choose the King James Version of this prayer simply because it is more poetic and is the one many of us memorized as children. The Scripture quotes in the rest of the lesson are taken from the New International version because it is translated from the original Greek/Hebrew language in more modern language.)

The Bible says that when even two or three people come together in His name (Jesus), that He is right here, too. We know that when we gather together in the name of Jesus, that He's right here with us, even though we can't see him. So, let's begin our lesson talking to God by saying what we like to call the "Lord's Prayer." It's an example of how we should pray.

> *Our Father, who art in Heaven,*
> *Hallowed by thy name.*
> *Thy/Your Kingdom come, thy/your will be done*
> *On earth as it is in Heaven.*
> *Give us this day our daily bread.*
> *And forgive us our debts (sins) as we forgive our debtors/those who sin against us.*
> *Lead us not into temptation,*
> *But deliver us from evil.*
> *For thine/yours is the Kingdom and the power, and the glory forever. Amen*

(While the last line is not evident in the earliest manuscripts, but was probably added later by a scribe, the thought is a good one, so we've included it in our prayer. Feel free to use it, or not, as the Spirit advises.)

The first thing to remember when teaching, either children or adults, is that the more they are encouraged and feel free to become involved, the more likely they are to listen, learn, and more importantly, remember.

- ❖ The cast

The A #1, most amazing, most powerful, smartest, wisest, most loving, most creative, most perfect Hero in the whole Bible, in fact in the whole world, is GOD!!! *The whole Bible, from beginning to end, is the story of God and who He is, the things He has done, and the promises He gives to those who love Him. The Bible is actually God's letter to us…and it's a <u>really</u> long letter.*

What do you think or know about God? (*Here are some sample questions. You may think of more you'd like to ask.*

a. Where does He live?
b. What does He do?
c. Does He ever lie?
d. Is there anything He can't do?
e. What do you think He looks like?
f. Can He ever die?

(Accept all answers, even if they miss the mark. The object of this lesson is not to see who is right or wrong, but to get children to thinking about who God is and who He is not, and they may be starting from a very sketchy foundation.)

Explain to the children that God has no body…no hands nor feet nor arms nor legs, etc… that He is a spirit, and help them to understand this concept.

Everyone in this room has a body, right? We all have heads and backs and other body parts. (Depending on the ages of your students, you might have them name other parts of their bodies <u>that everyone can see</u>.) *And since we have bodies, we have shapes. Basketballs have what kind of shape? (round) What kind of shapes do boxes have? (square, rectangle, etc.) Often we can identify an object simply by the shape of it.*

A fun activity is to gather up some commonly used objects, keeping them hidden from the children. (It's good to have at least one object per child in the class. Without them seeing the objects, put one object at a time into a cloth bag (pillow case, etc.) and allow each child to have a turn trying to guess just from the feel of the object what it is.

Say something like: *You did a great job recognizing what these things were just by looking at (or feeling) their shapes. Do you think we could put God in this bag and tell that it was God just by feeling His shape? (no, of course not.) Why not? Because God has no shape. In fact, God, the Father, has no body!!! We can't even see Him.*

So, how can we know He is real if we can't see Him? Can you think of anything that you know is real but that you can't see?

(The children may need a little prompting here…This little object lesson might help.)

(**Option 1**) Show the children both balloons and ask what the difference is between them. The difference is, of course, obvious. Then ask why one is flat and the other isn't. They will know, of course that the inflated balloon has air in it. You might ask how they know there is air in the balloon. Ask if they think they can see the air inside the balloon. If they say, "Yes," pop the balloon and ask if anyone saw the air that came out. They might have felt it and heard the sound it made when the balloon popped, but they couldn't see it.

(**Option 2**)Another way to illustrate the fact that although air is real and we can feel it, we can't see it…give each child a drinking straw and a plastic pony bead (Those with flat sides work better and are less likely to roll.)

You might say: *Let's play a little game. I'm going to give each of you a straw and a bead. When you get your straw, hold it still in one hand and place the bead on the table right in front of you. When I say, "go," try to move the bead by blowing on it through your straw. Don't let your straw touch the bead. Let's see who can move his bead the farthest while I count to 5 (or 10).*

After each child has succeeded in moving his/her bead, you can ask if anyone could see the air that was coming through the straw. When they respond, "no," you can ask them how they knew the air was there. (Because the bead moved.)

You can say, *Just like we could see our beads moving when we blew on them, we can see trees moving in the wind, but can we see the air that makes them move? Air is just one of the things that we know is real but that we can't see. Can you think of other things? What about thoughts, or feelings like love, anger, hunger, ideas, imagination, creativity, etc….(the list can go on and on…)*

When the children have exhausted their imaginations on this subject, or when you feel like it's time to move on, continue. (If children give incorrect answers here, it might be best to gently correct them, perhaps by asking them questions.)

Often we can recognize things just by their shapes. Hold up figures 1 and 2 and let the children tell you what each object is.

As we said, God has no shape, so we can't draw a picture of Him. We can't see God because He is a Spirit, and we can't see spirits. And it's a really good thing that He has no body. If God had a body, He could be in only one place at one time. For example, you can be here in this classroom, or you can be at your home. You can be at school or on a boat. But can you be in both places at once? Of course not. But God can be many different places at one time because He isn't limited by a body to either space or time.

So, if we can't see Him, how can we know that He is real? That's a really good question. Let's see if we can figure this one out.

If a new kid came to school and you wanted to know something about him, or her, you might want to know if he or she might be a good friend. What would you look for; what would you listen for? (...the way he acted, whether he was kind or mean, whether he was helpful, whether he shared or was selfish, how he talked to other people, whether he was funny, whether he liked to be around people or was a little, or a lot, shy....)

Learning all these things would help you get to know the new student. In the same way, we can know who God is without being able to see Him. One way is that we can look around us at the world He made. What are some things we can see and hear outside that show us something about God?

(The heavens, the clouds, the billions of stars, the beauty of the seasons, all the thousands of animals He created...looking at some of the animals would also help us believe that God has a sense of humor☺.)

We can know other things about God, too, and those are some of the things we're going to be talking about as we read Bible stories about some VERY interesting people.

Like we said before, God is a Spirit. Let's see what the Bible says about who God is...

(With older children, this is a good time to start teaching them about where to find things in the Bible. Help the children find John 4:23. Ask them to put a finger on the verse when they've found it.)

❖ *The Catch*

The fourth chapter of John, the 23rd and 24th verses say:

> "The time is coming and has now come when the true worshipers will worship the Father in Spirit and truth, for they are the kind of worshipers the Father seeks. God is spirit, and his worshipers must worship in spirit and in truth."

Memory verse: **John 4:24 God is spirit, and those who worship him must worship him in spirit and in truth. KJV**

(This is a good time to introduce the memory verse for today and help the children learn it. I've found it effective to help them learn the verses in phrases instead of one word at a time. We want them to remember the essence of the Word, not just to remember which word comes after the one before it. For example:

Please repeat after me: God is spirit, (children repeat a couple of times)
                    and those who worship him   " "
                    must worship him in spirit and in truth. " "

Once the children have mastered each phrase, help them learn to put it together along with the Bible reference. John 4:24

And since God is a spirit and has no body or shape, we can't draw or paint a picture of Him or make a statue of Him. Each of us is a spirit, too. And our bodies are the houses our spirits live in. We aren't bodies with spirits, we are actually spirits wrapped up in bodies.

- ❖ The feast

If time allows, this is a good time to offer the students snacks. While they are eating, you can gently review them on what they learned today. This should be enough to fill the classroom time. If not, you might give each child a balloon and ask the children to blow up their balloons. Batting them around the room is a good energy release and may also serve to help them understand the concept that many things are real, even though we can't see them.

Blessings to you and your children.

Figure 1

Figure 2

Figure 3

Thank you for sharing your child with us today. In class we talked about things that we know are real even if we can't see them, things like air and ideas, etc. We also learned that God is a Spirit.

Thank you for sharing your child with us today. In class we talked about things that we know are real even if we can't see them, things like air and ideas, etc. We also learned that God is a Spirit.

Thank you for sharing your child with us today. In class we talked about things that we know are real even if we can't see them, things like air and ideas, etc. We also learned that God is a Spirit.

Thank you for sharing your child with us today. In class we talked about things that we know are real even if we can't see them, things like air and ideas, etc. We also learned that God is a Spirit.

Thank you for sharing your child with us today. In class we talked about things that we know are real even if we can't see them, things like air and ideas, etc. We also learned that God is a Spirit.

Thank you for sharing your child with us today. In class we talked about things that we know are real even if we can't see them, things like air and ideas, etc. We also learned that God is a Spirit.

LET'S GO FISHING, LESSON 2
The Creation: Days 1-3

For your spirit:

> It's easy to skim over the Creation Story because most of us have heard it so many times. But in the first chapter of Genesis, we find evidences of the unfathomable POWER of God, His DESIRE to bring order out of chaos, His incomprehensible INTELLECT, His all-encompassing WISDOM, the AUTHORITY of His Word, the VITALITY and HUMOR of His CREATIVITY, and His COMMAND of sequence and order. In the very first book of the Bible we find God's first revelation of Himself to mankind. Ask God to reveal Himself and His truths as you study these Scriptures.

To the teacher: There are very few lessons (truths) in the Bible that are more fun to teach and more important to know than the story of Creation.

This is a rather long lesson; you may choose to divide it into two sessions.

Scripture reference: Genesis 1:1-13

Memory verse: "***In the beginning, God created the heavens and the earth***." Genesis 1:1

Emphasis: The power of God's Word…He spoke the world into being.

Supplies needed:

- A Bible for each child
- Dry-erase board and markers
- Paper (white, so the colors will be true), artist paper, copy paper, etc. for yourself (unless you'd rather use the dry-erase board) and each child, (whatever size works for the class size and table space.)
- Pencils for each child
- If you have access to the flannel graph creation story, that's a really good visual

- Music source: DVD, CD, or YouTube for "My God Is So Big"/ *Creation Song* by Saddleback Kids, *How God Made Everything* by Intellectual Baby (or Storytime DVD), or *7 Days of Creation* by GECD (for younger children)
- Building materials (blocks, Play-doh, modeling clay, etc.)
- Optional: a globe
- Optional, but often helpful…a kitchen timer
- Snacks (crackers and cheese?)
- Enough copies of the "Notes to the parents" addendum for each child to get one (Figure 9)
- Flannelgraph of the story of Creation, if you're using it

Teacher prep:
1. Pray for each child
2. Pray for yourself and any assistants you may have in your class.
3. Be prepared… Read through the Scriptures slowly and carefully, asking God to reveal His truths to you as you go. It may be tempting to rush through the verses, but doing that may cause us to miss some very important revelations. Also, familiarity with the teaching sequences will make your classes run more smoothly. Know your lesson and its emphasis well so you can tell it with only occasional glances at your notes. Also be familiar with the songs.
4. Snacks (optional)…many classes like to offer snacks during the Sunday School session. I've found that it usually works better if snack time is saved for the end of class. When it's offered at the beginning, it's often more difficult to move into the lesson.

Welcome each child as he/she enters. When the children have all found their places at the table, ask them to repeat the Lord's Prayer with you. If they aren't familiar with the words, you can write them on the dry-erase board or print them on a poster board to keep in your room. You may want to explain that it is important to invite God into the classroom by speaking to Him each morning.

Our Father, who art in Heaven,
hallowed by thy name.

Thy/Your Kingdom come, thy/your will be done
on earth as it is in Heaven.
Give us this day our daily bread,
and forgive us our debts (sins) as we forgive our debtors/those who sin against us.
Lead us not into temptation,
but deliver us from evil.
For thine/yours is the Kingdom and the power, and the glory forever. Amen

Review the previous lesson: ask the children what we learned about God. (that He is a spirit and has no body. Remind them of the memory verse and ask them to repeat it. ("*God is spirit, and His worshipers must worship {Him} in spirit and in truth."* John 4:24) Please remember that we want them to remember the thought of the Scripture, not necessarily word by word. So if they skip a word or use a synonym or add a word, it's OK as long as they retain the essence of it.

- ❖ The lure

    Music*: "My God Is So Big"/ "Creation Song" by Saddleback Kids, How God Made Everything by Intellectual Baby (or Storytime DVD), or 7 Days of Creation by GECD (for younger children)*

Provide building materials to the children and encourage them to build anything they would like to build. Alert them to the fact that they will have three-to-five minutes to complete what they are making. (Set the timer?)

At the end of this "construction" time, compliment the children on their projects and ask them to return the materials they used into whatever containers they belong.

Then say something like this: *Almost everyone likes to make things. That's called being "creative," and we do it because we were made in God's image, to be like God. Our God is creative and likes to make things, too. But our God can do something we can't do; He creates beautiful, wonderful things out of <u>nothing</u>.*

Cup your hands and offer the children a handful of nothing. Ask them what they could make with it. You might even give each child his/her share of "nothing."

The word for "create" in this passage means to make something out of nothing. I can't do this, can you? (You might give some examples of what we can't do with our words that God can do…for example…God said "Let there be light," and there was light. We can strike a match or light a candle or turn on a flashlight or flip and switch, but we cannot make light.)

Pass out the Bibles and help the children find the first chapter of Genesis. Have them put their fingers on chapter 1, verse 1.

❖ The cast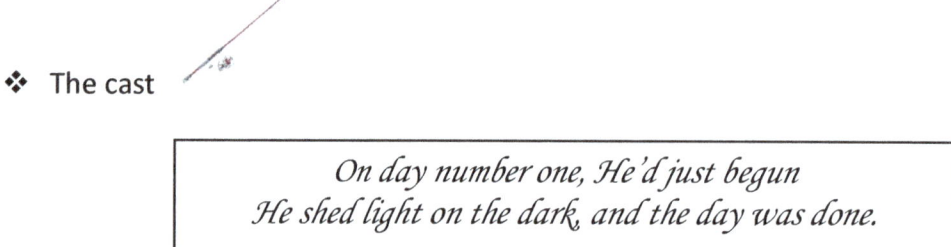

> *On day number one, He'd just begun*
> *He shed light on the dark, and the day was done.*

Say something like: *Today we're going to learn some things about our amazing God and some wonderful things He did. Let's all read the first verse together:*

If your children are old enough to read, encourage one child to read aloud while others follow along. If not, read it to them while they try to follow with their eyes.

Memory verse: **"In the beginning, God created the heavens and the earth."** Genesis 1:1

The verse says "in the beginning," in the beginning of what? (time) *In Heaven there is no such thing as time. The beginning of the creation of the world was also the beginning of time.*

Who was already there at the beginning? (God) *That's right; before the world ever began, God was already there. That's an important thing to remember…God had no beginning, and He has no end. He always was, and He always will be.*

And what did He do in the beginning? (created the heavens and the earth.)

The next verses we will explore will tell us about some of the things He created. Let's see what the second verse says to us...

> Verse 2:*"Now the earth was formless and empty, darkness was over the surface of the deep, and the Spirit of God was hovering over the waters.*

The earth didn't have a definite shape like it does now. It wasn't round or square or egg-shaped, and there was nothing to see on it except water.
When the Bible uses the words, "the deep" it is talking about water. So, basically, if the world was all water, then it wasn't anything like it is today.

(This is a good place to show them the globe and talk about how it looks now.)

It was really just a big, ugly, wet, dark blob! God didn't like that. We can imagine that He might have thought something like… "What a mess! Let's see what we can do with it."
Does your mother ever come into your room and say something like that? What needs to be done?

Notice that the Bible says that the Spirit of God was "hovering" over the waters. What does it mean to hover? (A lot of children will be familiar with hover crafts or hover boards. If not, you may say it's something like a helicopter or a hummingbird can do. I love to act this part out with my arms extended, like they are hovering over the table.)

Aha! Can you tell that something is about to happen...that God is fixing to make some changes? Let's read further and see what He did next.

> Verses 3, 4, 5: *And God said, "Let there be light," and there was light. God saw that the light was good, and He separated the light from the darkness. God called the light, "day," and the darkness He called "night." And there was evening and there was morning… the first day.*

So, what was the first thing God did to this dark, shapeless blob that was covered with water? (He created light and separated it from the darkness, making the first day and the first night. You might want to write down the number of the days and what was created on each one on the dry-erase board.) Show them **figure 4**.

Figure 4

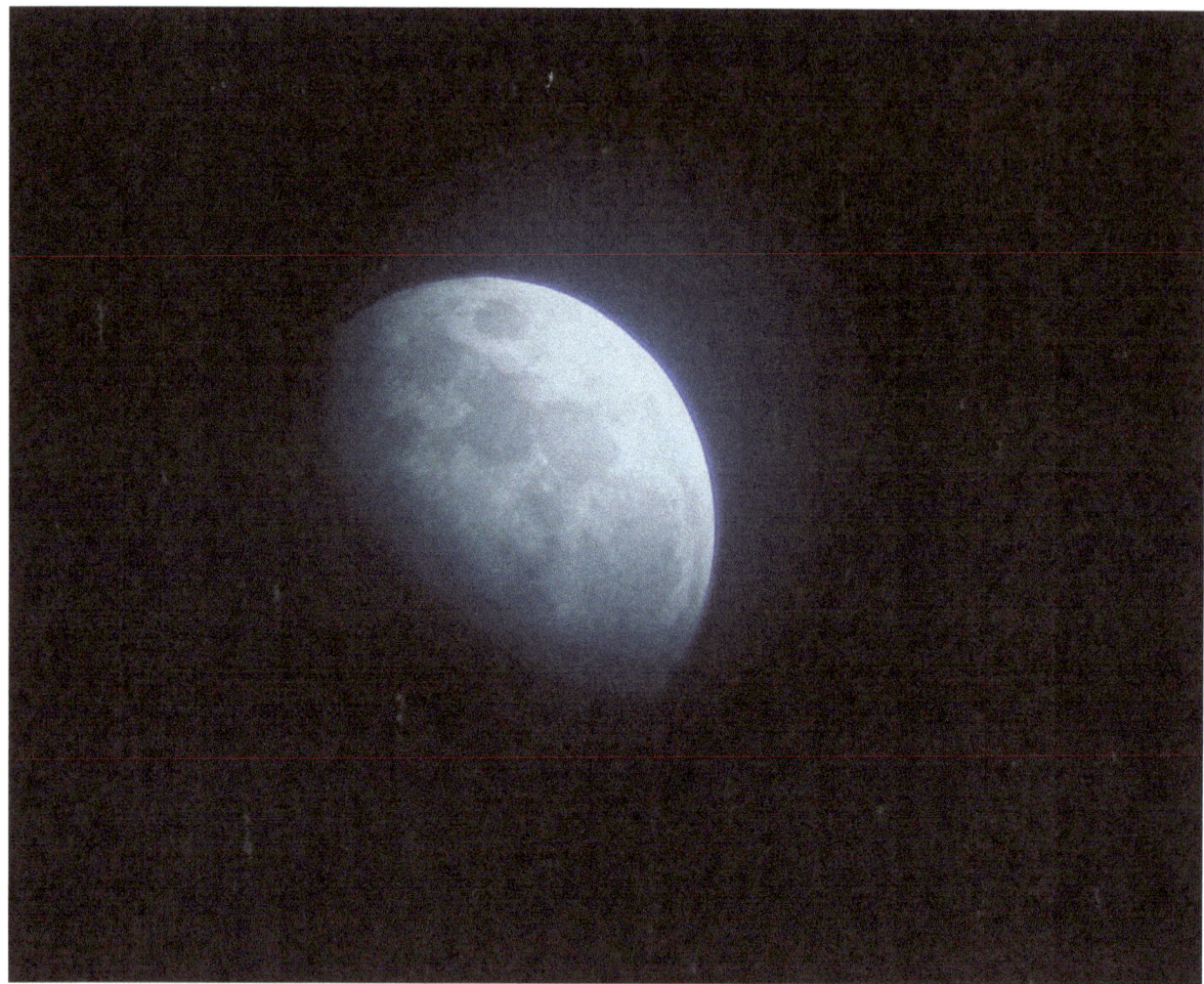

Photo by Beverly O'Malley

(Verse three is tricky, but <u>please</u> don't try to explain it away or slide over it or pretend that it doesn't say what it does say.)

Now, let's see what God did next.

> *On day number two He made the sky and wedged it between the waters way up high.*

Verses 6,7,8: *And God said, "Let there be an expanse between the waters to separate water from water."* <u>*So God made the expanse and separated the water under the expanse from the water over it*</u>*. And it was so. God called the expanse, "sky." And there was evening and there was morning...the second day.*

Whoa! Wait a minute! What did that say? Listen closely now...I'm going to tell you something that very few people in the world know about...but it's right here in the Bible, so we can believe that it's true.

 "And God said, "Let there be an expanse (a space) between the waters to separate water from water." That sounds like a sky "sandwich," doesn't it? There was water on the earth, and then God put the sky in between the water <u>on</u> the earth and the water that was <u>above</u> the earth.

(Show the picture of the two areas of water divided by the sky. {**Figure 5**. It appears at the end of the lesson} It will help the children get the idea if you draw this on the dry-erase board. Don't worry, when we study Noah, we'll find out what happened to that water.)

If you know anything about space, you know that there isn't any water above the sky now. If we got into a rocket ship and flew through space, we wouldn't have to worry about getting wet! So, if it's not there now, that means that something must have happened to it. Remember this; it's important...when we read about Noah and the ark, we'll find out what happened to that water that was above the sky.

Now, let's read verses 9 and 10 to see what happened on the third day.

> *He made the land on day number three,*
> *along with every flower and bush and tree.*

Have the children locate the following verses, beginning with verse 9. If you have those who can read and want to, encourage them to do so, one verse per child.

26

Verses 9, 10: "And God said, "Let the water under the sky be gathered to one place, and let dry land appear." And it was so. (v.10) God called the dry ground, "land," and the gathered waters he called "seas." And God saw that it was good.

So, what did He do next? (gathered the water together to make the seas, or oceans, and made dry ground appear.

Figure 6

Okay, so now we have light and dark, air (in the sky) and dry ground. See, God was planning ahead for what He wanted to do next.

This is a good place to discuss Pangea: (**figure 7**) There is a lot of evidence to suggest that all the earth was gathered together in one place in the beginning. As the oceans separated due to shifts of the earth's tectonic plates, the continents gradually drifted apart. (**Figures 7 & 8**)How long this process took is anybody's guess, but I'm an advocate of the theory that the earth isn't nearly as old as scientists seem to think. However, that is not the point. I think the children will find the maps below interesting.

Figure 7

Wikipedia commons

figure 8

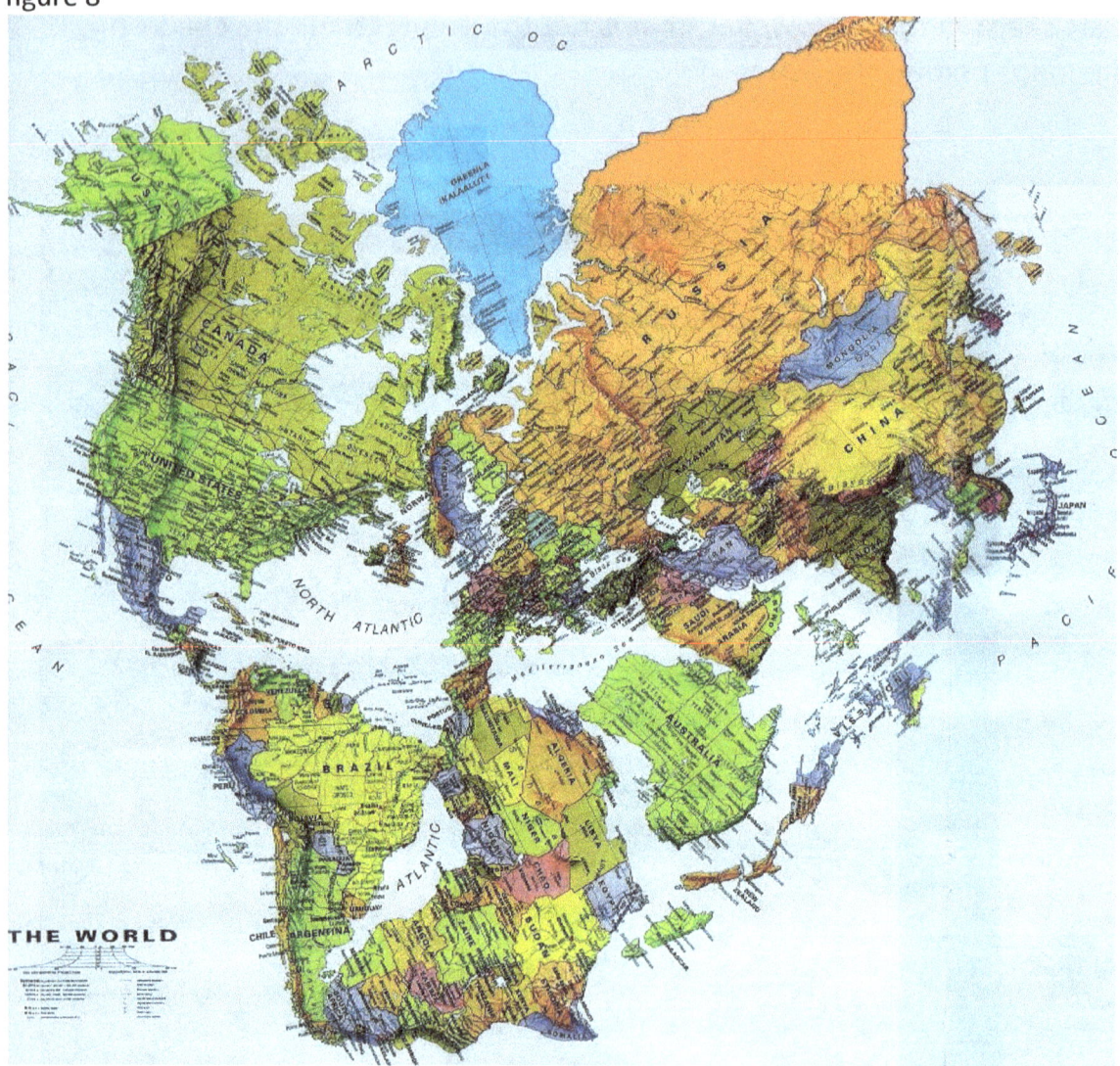

Joe Schiller

(v.11)
Then God said, "Let the land produce vegetation, seed-bearing plants and trees on the land that bear fruit with seed in it, according to their various kinds. And it was so......And God saw that it was good. And there was evening and there was morning-- the third day.

So, on the third day of creation what else did God make? (plants) *Can you see what He was doing? After He made the dry ground, He created all kinds of plants to grow on the ground. What kinds can you name?* (flowers, trees of all kinds, grass, vines, etc.)

Figure 9

Photo by Chance Agrella

Whew! All this creating is making me tired. Let's review our memory verse from yesterday and learn a new one for today.

(It's good to have these printed out or written on a dry-erase board.)

<u>John 4:24: God is spirit, and those who worship him must worship him in spirit and in truth. KJV</u>

<u>In the beginning, God created the heavens in the earth. Genesis 1:1</u>

Repeat after me: In the beginning
God created
The heavens and the earth. Genesis 1:1

- ❖ The catch

Activity time:

Hand out paper and pencils. As you demonstrate, either on paper or on the dry-erase marker board, ask the children to draw the land-, sea-, and sky-scape (with ocean, land and sky to begin with.) Then ask them to add plants…trees, flowers, etc. Explain that you'll add other things in the next lesson. (This is <u>a drawing time only</u>…coloring or painting will come after the drawing is completed at the end of lesson #3…or lesson #4 if you want them to add people to the drawing.)

- ❖ The feast

Snack suggestion: Let the kids "build" their own snacks with crackers and cheese.

Figure 5

Figure 9…Note to parents:

Thank you for sharing your child with us today. We learned some amazing facts about the first three days of creation. The memory verse for this week is: "In the beginning, God created the heavens and the earth." Genesis 1:1

Thank you for sharing your child with us today. We learned some amazing facts about the first three days of creation. The memory verse for this week is: "In the beginning, God created the heavens and the earth." Genesis 1:1

Thank you for sharing your child with us today. We learned some amazing facts about the first three days of creation. The memory verse for this week is: "In the beginning, God created the heavens and the earth." Genesis 1:1-13

Thank you for sharing your child with us today. We learned some amazing facts about the first three days of creation. The memory verse for this week is: "In the beginning, God created the heavens and the earth." Genesis 1:1-13

Thank you for sharing your child with us today. We learned some amazing facts about the first three days of creation. The memory verse for this week is: "In the beginning, God created the heavens and the earth." Genesis 1:1-13

Thank you for sharing your child with us today. We learned some amazing facts about the first three days of creation. The memory verse for this week is: "In the beginning, God created the heavens and the earth." Genesis 1:1-13

Thank you for sharing your child with us today. We learned some amazing facts about the first three days of creation. The memory verse for this week is: "In the beginning, God created the heavens and the earth." Genesis 1:1-13

LET'S GO FISHING, LESSON 3
The Creation: Days 4-5, Genesis 1:14-23

For your spirit:

> Psalm 104:1-25...*Praise the Lord, O my soul. O Lord my God, you are very great; you are clothed with splendor and majesty. He wraps himself in light as with a garment: he stretches out the heavens like a tent and lays the beams of his upper chambers on their waters. He makes the clouds his chariot and rides on the wings of the wind. He makes winds his messengers, flames of fire his servants. He set the earth on its foundations; it can never be moved. You covered it with the deep as with a garment; the waters stood above the mountains. But at your rebuke the waters fled, at the sound of your thunder, they took flight; they flowed over the mountains, and went down into the valleys, to the place you assigned for them. You set a boundary they cannot cross; never again will they cover the earth...*(please continue reading, at least to verse 25.)

Scripture reference: Genesis 1: 14-23

Memory verse: "**_The heavens declare the glory of God_**." Psalm 19:1

Emphasis: God made everything in the whole universe.

Supplies needed:

- Pencils and the creation drawings that the children started from the previous lesson
- Music: "How Great Is Our God" (Maranatha Singers/ Hillsong United/ Don Moen {You tube or from *With a Thankful Heart* album};
  or "My God Is So Big" by #One Love#Bless you#Peace, by Jeeva, 1996/ **or** Cedarmont Kids DVD
- Bible for each child
- Flannel Graph of Creation Story if you're using it
- Dry-erase board and markers
- Memory verse printed on paper or dry-erase board
- Figures #10-19
- Copies of the note to parents for each child (figure 19)

34

Teacher prep... please be completely familiar with the above scriptures as well as the illustrations.

Welcome each child. If some are in the habit of arriving considerably earlier than the others, please have an activity ready...an easy game or color page. (**figure #18**)

- ❖ The lure

Music: "How Great is our God" and/or "My God Is So Big"

The Lord's Prayer

Review of lessons 1 & 2, including memory verses

Hand out (or have the students hand out) the Bibles and turn to Genesis, chapter 1: verse 14. Ask the children to put their index fingers on the verse when they've found it.

We've talked about the things God created on the first, second, and third days of creation. Now, let's see what He's "got up His sleeve."(☺ God doesn't really have sleeves.)

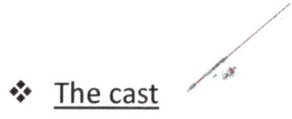

- ❖ The cast

Read, or ask one of the children to read verses 14-15.

> And God said, "Let there be lights in the expanse of the sky to separate the day from the night, and let them serve as signs to mark the seasons and days and years, and let them be lights in the expanse of the sky to give light on the earth. And it was so."

> *On day four he made two great lights*
> *to rule the sky on days and nights.*

So what is God going to do here? (make lights to put up in the sky) *And what does the Bible say about why He wanted to put lights up in the sky?* (to separate the day from the night).

And what else are the sun and the moon going to do? (They are going to mark the seasons and days and years.) *Okay...how is the sun going to mark the days? What do the sun and the moon have to do with a day?* (The sun comes up in the morning and goes down at night. The moon comes up and night and goes away in the morning.

{We know that in reality that it's the rotation of the earth that makes it <u>appear</u> like it's the sun and the moon that are moving when actually it's the earth spinning on its axis.. In any case, these two heavenly bodies are directly connected with the passing of days. And one complete circle around the sun marks the end of a year.

How does the sun affect the seasons, like winter, spring, summer, and fall? (It's warmer/hotter...late spring, summer, early fall...when the sun's rays are shining <u>more</u> directly on our part of the earth, and cooler/colder...late autumn, winter, early spring...when the sun's rays are shining less directly, more at an angle, on our part of the planet.)

Let's read some more: Let's find the 16th verse; please put your finger on the verse when you've found it.

Genesis 1: 16-19:

> *"God made two great lights—the greater light to govern the day and the lesser light to govern the night. He also made the stars. God set them in the expanse of the sky to give light on the earth, to govern the day and the night, and to separate light from darkness. And God saw that it was good. And the evening and the morning were the fourth day."*

Don't you find it interesting that God made light and separated it from the darkness before He made the sun and the moon? Have you ever been out at night, maybe out in the country or on a camping trip, away from the lights of town, and seen all the stars?

Did you know that our sun is actually a star? And it isn't even one of the bigger stars. All the planets that circle our sun, including the earth we live on, are a part of a solar (sun) system. Our solar system is part of a huge galaxy.

Do you know what a galaxy is? It is a system of millions or billions or stars held together by gravity. The galaxy we live in is called the Milky Way. (This is a good place to show the photo of the Milky Way.)

Figure 10

Universe today.com

The Milky Way (our galaxy…stars and their planets and meteors, and dust particles, etc. that are held together by magnetic attraction.)

There are literally billions and billions of stars and more than 100 billion galaxies. A billion is a thousand millions….that's a LOT of stars!

How long did it take Him to make the sun and the moon and all the stars? (one day) *That was a lot of creating to do in just one day. And did you know that the Bible also says that God calls all the stars by name? Pretty amazing God we have, isn't it? So, if God knows the names of the stars, do you think He knows our names, too?*

Memory verse: <u>***The Heavens declare the glory of God***</u>. **Psalm 19:1**

Ask the children to repeat the memory verse several times until they are comfortable with it and can say it with ease.

Figure 11

pbs. Org   The Universe:
(Universe…all existing things, the whole creation, consisting of all the stars and planets and galaxies, etc.)

Figure 12

Commons wikipedia   Comparative sizes of the earth and the moon

Figure 13

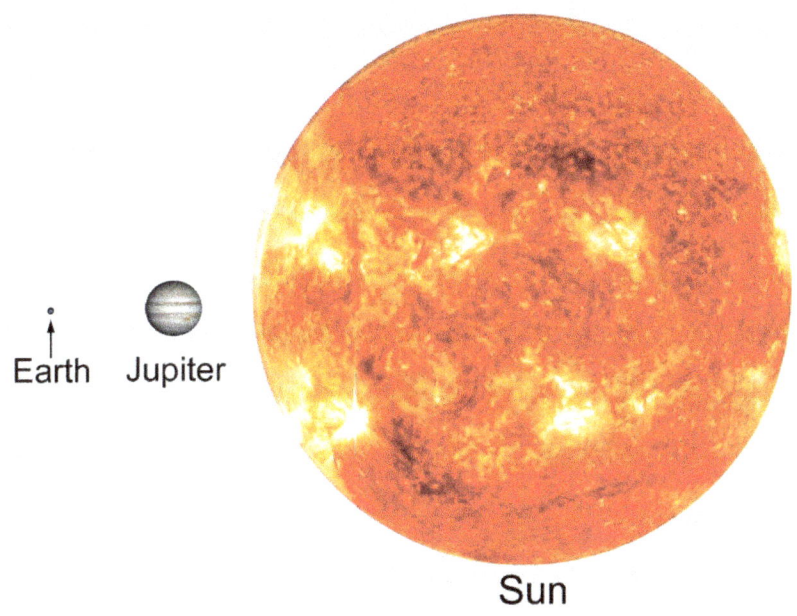

Clip art wiki Comparative sizes of the sun and the earth

So, by the end of the 4th day, God had separated the light from the dark, created an area (expanse) that He called the sky and wedged it in between the water that covered the earth and the water that was above the earth. He had gathered the waters on the earth together and called up the dry land. Then He told the land to bring forth plants. And after that he set up the heavens, with the sun and moon and all the stars. He did all that in four days...boy, was He busy!!!

Now let's find verse 20 in our Bibles and see what God had in His mind to make on the fifth day.

> *He made the birds and every fish alive to fill the air and the seas on day number five.*

v. 20... And God said, "Let the water teem with living creatures, and let birds fly above the earth across the expanse of the sky.

v. 21... So God created the great creatures of the sea and every living and moving thing with which the water teems, (*"teem" means "to be full of."*) *according to their kinds, and every winged bird according to its kind. And God saw that it was good.*

v. 22...And God blessed them and said, "Be fruitful and increase in number and fill the water in the seas, and let the birds increase on the earth." And there was evening and there was morning, the fifth day.

Now we're getting to the fun stuff! I'll bet God had a blast when He was designing all the beautiful and strange-looking fish and birds, don't you? Let's take a look at just a few of the millions of different kinds of fish and birds that He created to fill the earth. What do you think the fact that He created so <u>many</u> different kinds of fish and birds says about God's character and personality? Do you think it shows that He was making a wonderful, exciting and colorful world to put His people in?

<u>**Figures 14-17**</u> show some the children might enjoy. <u>**Figure 18**</u> is a color page.

- ❖ <u>The catch</u>

Hand out drawings from the previous lesson and ask the children to add the sun and the moon and stars. Then they can draw some fish and birds. While they are drawing, ask them what seeing God's creation tells us about Himself. (Creative, imaginative, good, wise, sense of humor...And it looks to me like He had FUN!)

- ❖ <u>The feast</u>

Snack time!

Figure 14

See-through sea cucumber

Squidworm

Christmas tree worm

sea angel

Armored snail

bioluminescent octopus

Figure 15

Fangtooth

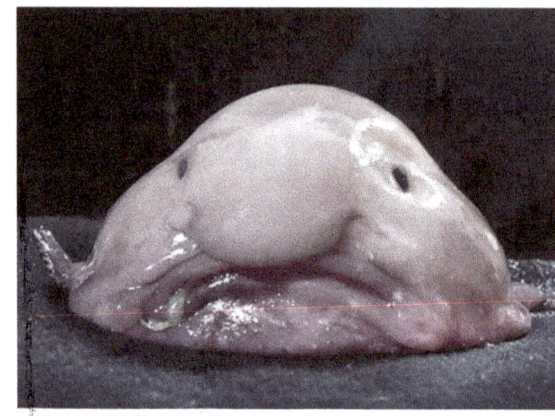

blob fish

Trigger fish

emperor angel fish

Mandarin fish

beta fish

Figure 16

King vulture

Philippine eagle

Inca tern

rhinoceros hornbill big horn

Long-wattled umbrella bird

chukar partridge

Figure 17

Victoria crowned pigeon

birds of paradise

Mandarin duck

golden pheasant

Peacock

peacock

Figure 18

Figure 19

Dear Parent: We enjoyed our class today. We learned how God spoke the sun, the moon, and the stars into existence and how He created the fish in the seas and the birds in the air.

Dear Parent: We enjoyed our class today. We learned how God spoke the sun, the moon, and the stars into existence and how He created the fish in the seas and the birds in the air.

Dear Parent: We enjoyed our class today. We learned how God spoke the sun, the moon, and the stars into existence and how He created the fish in the seas and the birds in the air.

Dear Parent: We enjoyed our class today. We learned how God spoke the sun, the moon, and the stars into existence and how He created the fish in the seas and the birds in the air.

Dear Parent: We enjoyed our class today. We learned how God spoke the sun, the moon, and the stars into existence and how He created the fish in the seas and the birds in the air.

Dear Parent: We enjoyed our class today. We learned how God spoke the sun, the moon, and the stars into existence and how He created the fish in the seas and the birds in the air.

Dear Parent: We enjoyed our class today. We learned how God spoke the sun, the moon, and the stars into existence and how He created the fish in the seas and the birds in the air.

LET'S GO FISHING, LESSON 4
The Creation of Land Animals, Genesis 1:24, 25 & 30, Job 41:14- 21

For your spirit:

> *"I lift up my eyes to the hills—Where does my help come from? My help comes from the Lord, the Maker of Heaven and earth. He will not let your foot slip—He who watches over you will not slumber."* Psalm 121:1, 2

Scripture reference: Genesis 1: 24-25, 30, Job 41:14-21

Memory verse: "**_For nothing is impossible with God_**."Luke 1:37

Emphasis: Please note that when He created land animals, He did not just speak them into being like He did the Heavens, the seas, and the land. He commanded the earth to bring forth the land animals.

Supplies needed:

- ➢ The children's unfinished pictures of the creation.
- ➢ Pencils & crayons or water colors. (If watercolors, aprons for each child, brushes, water, and paper towels.)
- ➢ A Bible for each child
- ➢ Music: "God Can Do Anything," or "Hallelu, Hallelu, Hallelu, Hallelujah!" (Cedarmont Kids), or "What a Mighty God We Serve" (Cedarmont Kids), "I'm Gonna Sing, Sing, Sing" (Cedarmont Kids)
- ➢ Figures 21-29
- ➢ Note to parents for each child (figure 29)
- ➢ Optional: Flannel Graph story

Teacher prep: Have everything you need ready for the class before it begins. Read the Scripture references through several times so that you are completely familiar with them. Make copies of "Note to Parents". Pray for the children, their families, and yourself. What we're striving for in this whole series of lessons is for God to become "real" for the children...so they will begin to think of Him as a vital, and welcome, part of their lives.

Welcome:

The lure

Music: (see above suggestions)

Lord's Prayer

Review of lessons 1, 2 & 3 including memory verses
> *God is spirit, and his worshipers must worship in spirit and in truth.* John 4:24
> *In the beginning, God created the heavens and the earth.* Genesis 1:1
> *The heavens declare the glory of God.* Psalm 19:1

The cast

Now, let's open our Bibles to the very beginning. We find the book of Genesis. The word, "Genesis," actually means "the beginnings." In this book we are finding out about the beginnings of the world…We're learning about how God made the sun and moon and stars, the seas and land, the plants, and the very first creatures of the sea (they're not all fish!) and the birds of the air. When we think of birds, what's the first thought we have? (They can fly) Can you think of any birds that do not actually fly? (penguins, ostriches, kiwis, etc.) (See figures 21, 22)

*Can you think of any creatures that live in the sea that aren't actually fish? All <u>fish</u> are cold-blooded animals that live in the water. They have backbones and fins, and get their oxygen through their gills. (*See figures 23, 24)

After seeing pictures of some of these animals, do you think you might understand some things about God? (That He is creative, imaginative, has a sense of humor, like beautiful things, etc.)

He made all these animals, the birds of the air and the creatures of the sea, on the fifth day. And now that we've learned about the birds and the sea animals that

God created, let's move on in our Bible reading to Genesis, Chapter 1, verses 24 and 25, and verse 30.

Read, or have the students read Genesis 1, verse 24.

> *"And God said, "Let the land produce living creatures according to their kinds: livestock, creatures that move along the ground, and wild animals, each according to its kind. And it was so."*

> *On day number six there was work to do;*
> *He made land animals two by two.*

So, what did He make next? (animals). *Let's notice something here. Did God just say, "Let there be animals" like He said about the sun and moon and stars, about light and sky? Look closely...He said, "<u>Let the land produce...</u>" This still shows us the power of His Word, but more than that, it shows us that He's the Lord of all He made...He's the boss; He can tell nature what to do. He told the land to produce living creatures, and it did. The land, itself, obeys its Creator. Everything in all Creation is under the authority of God, the Creator. Cool, huh? He can tell the winds to blow, the clouds to rain, the grass to come up, the flowers to bloom, etc. He can also tell them NOT to do those things. He can tell the rains to stop, the winds not to blow. In one place in the Bible, He made the sun stop traveling across the sky for one whole day!* (Joshua 10: 12-14)*There is absolutely NOTHING He cannot do if He wants to.*

So far, everything He has made obeys Him. It has no choice. Nature does what God tells it to. But soon we'll learn about something He made that has a choice, that can choose to obey God, or not to. What do you think that is?

But for right now let's talk for just a few minutes about the divisions of animals that the Bible listed. First He made what? (livestock). *Does anybody know what livestock is?* (animals kept or raised for use or pleasure especially: farm animals kept for use and profit) *I'll bet you can tell me some of the animals you might find on a farm.* (Give the children time to respond. If they mention something like skunks or snakes, you can redirect them by saying that these are wild animals and

50

that people don't usually raise these kinds of animals on purpose.) Figure 25 shows animals that are considered "livestock."

The Bible also says he made creeping things and wild animals. (Figures 26-28 show different kinds of wild animals, including dinosaurs.)
Let's read verse 30 to see what God provided for these animals to eat.
> "And to all the beasts of the earth and all the birds of the air and all the creatures that move on the ground—I give every green plant for food."

So what kind of food did God provide for all the animals? (Plants) *Notice that in the beginning, animals did not eat other animals.*

There's one last thing we need to find in our Bibles today. (Help the children find the 41st chapter of Job, verse 1. Ask them to put their fingers on the verse when they have found it.) . When they have read verse 1, skip down to verse 14. Read, or have the children read the whole passage at one reading...not verse by verse as we have done previously.
> *Can you pull in the leviathan with a fishhook or tie down his tongue with a rope?...Verses 14-21...Who dares open the doors of his mouth, ringed about with his fearsome teeth? His back has rows of shields tightly sealed together, each so close to the next that no air can pass between. (Skip v. 17)...His snorting throws out flashes of light; his eyes are like the rays of dawn. Firebrands stream from his mouth; sparks of fire shoot out. Smoke pours from his nostrils as from a boiling pot over a fire of reeds. His breath sets coals ablaze, and flames dart from his mouth.*

What kind of animal does that sound like to you? (a dragon?) *Cool, huh?*

The catch

Show the pictures on figures 26, 27, 28 and then invite them to complete their drawings, adding whatever animals they would like. Allow them plenty of time even if this activity continues into the next lesson. If time permits, allow them to begin their paintings, encouraging them to take their time and do a good job. They can snack while they draw and paint. (Hint: If they use crayons to color the individual items they've drawn…plants, sun, moon, animals, etc…they can use watercolors to paint the sky and foreground. The crayon prevents the paint from penetrating or sticking to the surface of the objects, so the effect is pretty cool.)

- ❖ <u>The feast</u>

Snack time!

Pass out the note to the parents, figure 29

figure 21

Cassowary from New Guinea and Australia

Penguin found only in Southern Hemisphere
Figure 22

Kiwi from New Zealand

Steamer duck from Chile and Argentina

Ostrich from Africa

Takahe from New Zealand

Figure 23

Octopus

Starfish

Figure 24

Whale

Dolphins

Clam

Figure 25

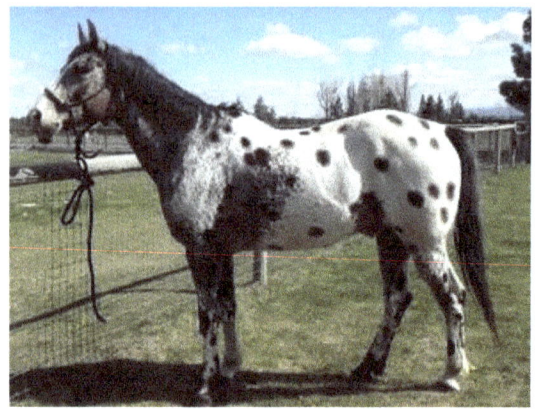

Figure 26

Figure 27

Figure 28

Figure 29

Dear Parent. Our Bible lessons are getting more and more interesting. We are learning about the Creation and the Creator and about how all of nature is under God's authority. The children are creating an artwork of their own and are looking forward to showing it to you.

Dear Parent. Our Bible lessons are getting more and more interesting. We are learning about the Creation and the Creator and about how all of nature is under God's authority. The children are creating an artwork of their own and are looking forward to showing it to you.

Dear Parent. Our Bible lessons are getting more and more interesting. We are learning about the Creation and the Creator and about how all of nature is under God's authority. The children are creating an artwork of their own and are looking forward to showing it to you.

Dear Parent. Our Bible lessons are getting more and more interesting. We are learning about the Creation and the Creator and about how all of nature is under God's authority. The children are creating an artwork of their own and are looking forward to showing it to you.

Dear Parent. Our Bible lessons are getting more and more interesting. We are learning about the Creation and the Creator and about how all of nature is under God's authority. The children are creating an artwork of their own and are looking forward to showing it to you.

Dear Parent. Our Bible lessons are getting more and more interesting. We are learning about the Creation and the Creator and about how all of nature is under God's authority. The children are creating artworks of their own and are looking forward to showing them to you.

LET'S GO FISHING, LESSON 5
Summary of the First Five Days & Introduction to the Bible (first four books)

For your spirit:

> Not to us, O Lord, not to us,
>   but to your name be the glory
>   because of your love and faithfulness. Psalm 115:1

B.O.B
(B.O.B can stand for "Big Old Book", "Book of Books", or "Books of the Bible")

Memory verse: "***The word of God is living and active and sharper than any two-edged sword.***" Hebrews 4:12 (English Standard Version)

Emphasis: God created the whole universe with the Word of His mouth.

Supplies needed:
- The children's unfinished artwork
- Pencils, crayons (or watercolors, aprons, water, paper towels, brushes, painter's palettes or individual watercolor palettes.)
- Music DVD's or CD's
- Illustrations from previous lessons for them to look at to help finish their art work
- Bibles for each child
- Copy of note to parents for each child, Figure 30
- Optional: a "clothes line" with clothes pins or other method of displaying their work

Teacher prep:
    Assemble art supplies
    Make copies of parent note, one for each child
    Snacks

Today will be a "catch-up" day. For those who haven't finished their artwork, this is a day to do it. Encourage them to be thoughtful and careful and take their time. Some will probably rush through it; the efforts of others may be painstakingly slow. For those who rush through it, there are several alternatives: If you have an accurate video of the Creation, this will be a good time to show it while others are finishing up their art work. (God*'s Creation according to Genesis* by Praiseshark; *Animated Bible Stories*: the Creation DVD)

(The delay in presenting the second half of Day 6, the creation of man, is intentional. We'll present it in two parts. The first lesson will be on the creation, itself, during which we'll attempt to explain as well as humans can, the concept of the Triune God. Please don't panic; we're not going into it too deeply, and we have a couple of easy-to-grasp illustrations to help them get an idea of the concept. But the children are old enough to be exposed to the idea that we worship One God, Who presents Himself in three forms…God, the Father, God, the Son, and God, the Holy Spirit. We'll also discuss the seventh day of Creation, when God rested from His labors.
In the second lesson in this two-part series, we'll talk about "The Fall" of mankind.)

When the children have all finished their art projects, we'll begin teaching them the books of the Bible (B.O.B)

Encourage them to repeat the previous memory verses. (It helps sometimes if you give them the first few words and let them complete the verse.)

> *"God is spirit, and those who worship him must worship in spirit and truth."* John 4:24
> "In the beginning, God created the heavens and the earth." Genesis 1:1
> *"For nothing is impossible with God."* Luke 1:37
> *"The heavens declare the glory of God."* Psalm 19:1

Memory verse: (learned in three parts)
> *The Word of God*
> *Is living and active*
> *and sharper than any two-edged sword. Hebrews 4:12*

As usual, when the children have mastered the three segments, encourage them to say the whole verse several times. This is a good time to pass out their Bibles.

****B.O.B****

What is the Word of God? Do we have it? Does this scripture say that the Word of God (as we find in the Bible) is dead, or alive? If the Bible just a lot of words on pages, or is it a place we can go to learn who God is and what He wants?

Our memory verse says the Word of God is sharper than any two-edged sword…Why would it be good to have a sword that is sharp on both edges?

And we've been learning about how God created the whole universe by the power of His Word.
So, let's take some time to get to know our Bibles.

The Bible is a book of books. That means that there are a lot of individual "books" in the Bible all joined together into one big book. Altogether, there were about 40 men who wrote the books of the Bible…we know some of their names; other books were written anonymously. That means we don't know who wrote them. Some men wrote only one book; some wrote several; and some books, like the Psalms were written by several different men.

The Bible is divided into two main sections: the Old Testament, and the New Testament.

The word "testament" means "covenant" or "agreement." The Old Testament talks about God's agreement with mankind before Jesus came into the world. (Remember that Jesus was in Heaven with God, the Father, and God, the Holy Spirit since before the beginning of time.) In the Old Testament God makes an agreement that says that <u>if people will obey His laws</u>, He will bless them and take care of them. That's why it is called the <u>Covenant of the Law</u>.

In the New Testament, God makes a new agreement with His people. It's called the Covenant of Grace, and we'll talk more about that later on.

There are 66 books in the Bible, 39 books in the Old Testament, or Covenant, and 27 books in the New Testament.

The very first book in the Bible is what? (Genesis) *We've been reading in Genesis about the creation of the world and, indeed, the whole universe. Can you open your bibles to the book of Genesis?*

Very good. The very last book in the Bible is the book of Revelation. Can you turn to the very end of your Bible and find that book?
Awesome…now let's have a little contest. Close your Bibles. Raise your hand if you know the name of the first book in the Bible. What is it? (Genesis)
Now, raise your hand if you know the name of the last book in the Bible. (Revelation)
Raise your hand if you remember how many main sections there are in the Bible. (2)
Raise your hand if you remember what they are called. (Old and New Testaments)

Now, since we know the names of the first and last books in the Bible, let's learn the names of the <u>first four books</u> in the Old Testament part of the Bible. It's so easy, just repeat after me.
       Genesis, Exodus, Leviticus, Numbers.

Have them repeat until they "have it". Then you can line the children up or have them form a circle, or gather into two teams. Then ask them to say the first four books in order, one book per child. After they've done this a few time, they should all be to repeat them in order.

If you have extra time, you might play a game. You'll need to have printed (by hand or on the computer) each book title on a separate slip of paper, one set for each team. (It's more colorful to use colored copy paper, but the kids might memorize the order of the colors instead of the names.)

Mix the order of the books and place them in two (or more, depending on the number of students in the class) piles, face down on a table. Divide the group into two or more teams and ask them to get into lines, first child at the head of the line, followed by others, in order.

Mark a starting line with masking tape. At your signal, each child, in turn, will run to the table and line the names in order. (You'll need to reshuffle the slips of paper after each contestant gets it correct. If you have a helper, it might be good to employ him/her to help with this to keep the game moving.)

Snacks...

God bless you and your children.

Figure 30

Good morning. Thank you for sharing your child with us today. We finished our "Creation" paintings and began learning about the Bible. Our memory verse was, "The word of God is living and active and sharper than any two-edged sword." Hebrews 4:12 Then we began learning the order of the books in the Bible. God bless and have a great week.

Good morning. Thank you for sharing your child with us today. We finished our "Creation" paintings and began learning about the Bible. Our memory verse was, "The word of God is living and active and sharper than any two-edged sword." Hebrews 4:12 Then we began learning the order of the books in the Bible. God bless and have a great week.

Good morning. Thank you for sharing your child with us today. We finished our "Creation" paintings and began learning about the Bible. Our memory verse was, "The word of God is living and active and sharper than any two-edged sword." Hebrews 4:12 Then we began learning the order of the books in the Bible. God bless and have a great week.

Good morning. Thank you for sharing your child with us today. We finished our "Creation" paintings and began learning about the Bible. Our memory verse was, "The word of God is living and active and sharper than any two-edged sword." Hebrews 4:12 Then we began learning the order of the books in the Bible. God bless and have a great week.

Good morning. Thank you for sharing your child with us today. We finished our "Creation" paintings and began learning about the Bible. Our memory verse was, "The word of God is living and active and sharper than any two-edged sword." Hebrews 4:12 Then we began learning the order of the books in the Bible. God bless and have a great week.

LESSON 6, THE CREATION OF MAN, THE TRIUNE GOD
Genesis 1:26-31

For your spirit:

> Lord, you have been our dwelling place throughout all generations. Before the mountains were born or you brought forth the earth and the world, from everlasting to everlasting you are God. Psalm 90:1-2

Scripture reference: Genesis 1:26-31; John 1:1-5, 14; 2 Corinthians 4:4

Memory Verse: *"**In the beginning was the Word, and the Word was WITH God, and the Word WAS God.**"* John 1:1 (Capital letters added for emphasis.)

Emphasis: *** This is one of the most important truths for children, and adults, to understand. Verse 14 of the first chapter of John states that "The Word became flesh and dwelt among us." Who was it that came down from Heaven and became "flesh"? The answer is simple but often overlooked…JESUS…He is the Word who became flesh and dwelt among us. So, in actuality, <u>Jesus is the Word of God</u>. He is God's message and God's truth, presented to us in human form so that we might be able to relate to and understand Him.

Please, please, please help your children to understand this. John 1:3 says that "Through him (the Word) all things were made; without him nothing was made that has been made." So, when God, the Father said, "Let us make man in <u>our</u> image," He was talking to God, the Son and to God, the Holy Spirit.

There are some sects that believe and teach that Jesus was a created being just like the angels. But this passage clearly states that He was there <u>in the beginning</u>! And, in its original language, the word for "God" in Genesis 1:1 is presented in its <u>plural</u> form.

Supplies:
- ➢ Bibles for each student

- Music: (Your choice) *Shout to the Lord* (PraiseBaby, Praises and Smiles CD); *Great is the Lord* (Praise Baby, God of Wonders CD): *My God is So Big* (Cedarmont Kids, vol.2); *What a Mighty God We Serve* (Cedarmont Kids, Vol. 2)
- Crayons
- Scissors for each child
- Invisible tape
- Figures 32 & 33—one for each child (fig. 32 can be copied on plain paper or card stock)
- A prepared triangular prism from figure 33 for an example
- Figure 31—note to parents
- Snacks

Teacher prep: Prayers for the children you teach, for yourself that God would guide you by His Spirit and give you wisdom and understanding beyond your own, and that the children's hearts and spirits will be open to receiving God's Truth.

Welcome:

❖ The lure

Music: (Your choice) "Shout to the Lord" (PraiseBaby, Praises and Smiles CD); "Great is the Lord" (Praise Baby, God of Wonders CD): "My God is So Big" (Cedarmont Kids, vol.2); "What a Mighty God We Serve" (Cedarmont Kids, Vol. 2)

❖ The cast

Pass out the Bibles as you encourage the children to remember the previous lesson(s).

I know that all of you remember what the first book of the Bible is called. (Genesis). *Does anyone remember what the word, "Genesis", means?* (Beginnings)

Very good! So, now, let's turn in our Bibles and find the first chapter of Genesis and look for verse 26. When you've found it, please place your index finger where the verse begins.

You may read the verses to them or have them read.
"Then God said, 'Let us make man in our image, in our likeness.'"

This is a good place to pause and make sure they understand what an image is.

*We can understand what an image is if we look into a mirror, what we see there isn't actually a person. If we reached out and touched it, it would feel hard, cold, and slick, not at all like our skin. It's an "image" of ourselves. (*Also, it's good to point out that, since God has no body, we weren't made to LOOK like Him.*) We were made with His attributes, or characteristics. We were made to have intelligence, a will, a spirit, a spiritual "heart", an imagination, creativity, faith, and a sense of humor. We were made to feel love and joy and anger and impatience and fear and compassion. (We can also be afraid, although fear doesn't come from God because He's not afraid of anything. When Adam and Eve were in the Garden of Eden, they had no fear. If they had, they might not have listened to the serpent.)*

Let's look at what that verse actually says. "Then God said, 'Let US make man in our image. To whom was He speaking? Obviously there were others there with Him because He wasn't talking to Himself. To whom do you think He was speaking? (Consider all answers before asking them to turn in their Bibles to <u>John 1:1</u>. I suggest you read these next Scriptures to them, asking them to follow along in the Bible as you read.)

"In the beginning was the Word, and the Word was WITH God, and the Word WAS God."

Wow! Who does this say was with God in the beginning? The WORD, right! Notice that the word, "Word," is capitalized. That means that it is the name of a particular person or thing. So, who, or what, is the Word, and what did He do?

Let's find verse 14 to find out who the Word was…

"The Word became flesh and made his dwelling (home) among us."

So, who do we know that came down from Heaven to live on earth? (Jesus). What this verse is telling us is that Jesus is the WORD of God. He is God's message to us. But even more importantly, verse 1 says the Word was with God, and the Word WAS God. So, Jesus was with God, and He was God at the very beginning.— before time even began. This may be hard for us to understand, but we'll talk more about that in a minute.

Let's look back up to verse 3 to find out what the Word (Jesus) did.

> *"Through him all things were made; without him nothing was made that has been made."*

So, when God created the world, Jesus was there with Him. And there was someone else who was there, too. It was the Holy Spirit. And when God said, "Let us make man in our image," He was talking to Jesus, and the Holy Spirit. Tricky, huh?

But now let's get back to the story of Creation in the first chapter of Genesis. We'll continue reading in verse 26.

> *Then God said, "Let us make man in our image, in our likeness, and let them rule over the fish of the sea and the birds of the air, over the livestock, over all the earth, and over all the creatures that move along the ground.*

Notice that God said, "Let them," not "let him."

> Verse 27: *So God created man in his own image, in the image of God he created him; male and female he created them.*

> Verse 28: *God blessed them and said, "Be fruitful and increase in number; fill the earth and subdue it. Rule over the fish of the sea and the birds of the air and over every living creature that moves on the ground."*

In verse 29, God tells the people He had made what He has provided for them to eat.

> *The God said, "I give you every seed-bearing plant on the face of the whole earth and every tree that has fruit with seed in it…*

Verse 31: **God saw all that he had made, and it was very good. And there was evening and there was morning—the sixth day.**

And on the seventh day God had finished creating the world and the universe, so He rested from his work.

There is something we need to know about God that is very hard for us to understand…

There is only one God, but there are three forms of God. They are: God, the Father, God the Son, and God the Holy Spirit.

One example that might help us understand this is to think about water. What do we know about water? (allow several responses…i.e. "it is wet, it can be hot or cold, it can move or be still, it can be on the land, in a river or lake, in a pipe, or fall from the sky."

Then ask: *Is water something we can stir with a stick or a spoon? Always? What if it's frozen? Then it's hard and we can't stir it, right? What happens if we put water in a pan and turn the heat on under it? Have you ever seen steam coming up from water when it gets very hot, or rising from the ground when the cold rain falls on the hot soil? Can you stir the steam? Of course not, but it is still water, just in another form. So we have water we can stir, water that is frozen into ice, and water that rises like gas into the air. But it's all still water.*

And God is sort of like that…He is in three different forms, but all the forms are still God.

❖ The catch

Another way to help us understand the "three-person" God is to think of a clover.

You may distribute copies of **figure 32** for the children to color (any pastel color they choose; really dark colors would cover the words.) Give them a minute or two to color their clover before moving on to the next project.

Another way to illustrate this idea of the triune (three-in-one) God is with the triangular prism in **figure 33**. Please prepare a completed triangle yourself before class to show the children what their goal should be. It will be easier if the children cut out the text rectangles first and glue them onto the small triangles surrounding the one in the center with the word "GOD" printed on it. Then they may either color or paint the figure before cutting it out. (They might enjoy coloring each triangle a different color. Once the figure is cut out, fold it on the lines to make a pyramid, being sure that the words are on the outside, not the inside ☺ and tape the edges together. This illustrates that, even though all the sides have different names, they are all God.

❖ The feast
Snacks

Figure 31

Dear Parents: Today we learned a little bit about how man was made in the image of God and about the Triune God...Our memory verse for today is "*In the beginning was the Word, and the Word was WITH God, and the Word WAS God.*" John 1:1

Dear Parents: Today we learned a little bit about how man was made in the image of God and about the Triune God...Our memory verse for today is "*In the beginning was the Word, and the Word was WITH God, and the Word WAS God.*" John 1:1

Dear Parents: Today we learned a little bit about how man was made in the image of God and about the Triune God...Our memory verse for today is "*In the beginning was the Word, and the Word was WITH God, and the Word WAS God.*" John 1:1

Dear Parents: Today we learned a little bit about how man was made in the image of God and about the Triune God...Our memory verse for today is "*In the beginning was the Word, and the Word was WITH God, and the Word WAS God.*" John 1:1

Dear Parents: Today we learned a little bit about how man was made in the image of God and about the Triune God...Our memory verse for today is "*In the beginning was the Word, and the Word was WITH God, and the Word WAS God.*" John 1:1

Dear Parents: Today we learned a little bit about how man was made in the image of God and about the Triune God...Our memory verse for today is "*In the beginning was the Word, and the Word was WITH God, and the Word WAS God.*" John 1:1

Figure 32

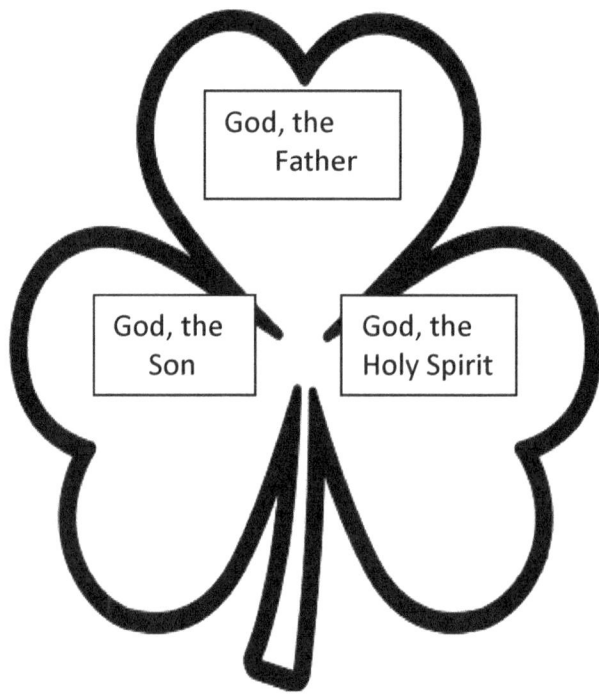

Figure 33

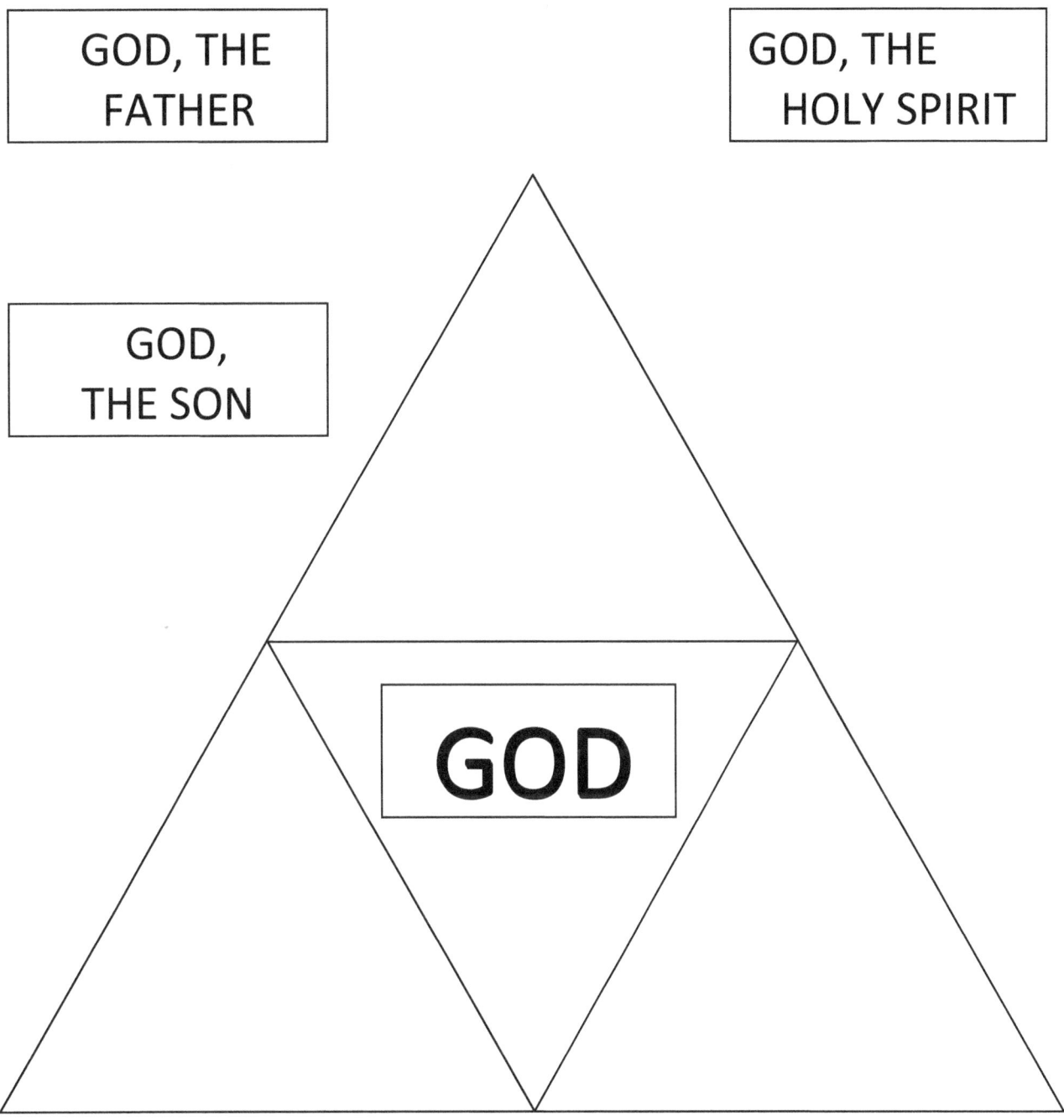

Triune God pyramid © Deana Carmack

LET'S GO FISHING, LESSON 7
The Creation of Man

For your spirit

> The weakest saint can experience the power of the Deity of the Son of God if we are willing to "let go." Any strand of our own energy will blur the life of Jesus. We have to keep "letting go," and slowly and surely the great full life of God will invade us in every part, and men will take knowledge of us that we have been with Jesus. Oswald Chambers

Scripture reference: Genesis 1:27; Genesis 2: 4-8, 15-22

Memory Verse: **Blessed are those who hear the word of God and obey it**. Luke 11:28

Emphasis: God provided everything people would need or want and gave them only one law—they were not to eat from the tree of the knowledge of good and evil. For if they did that, they would die.

Supplies needed:
- A Bible for each student
- Crayons, colored pencils or markers
- Coloring page for each student (figure 34)
- Modeling clay
- Wax paper (to work the clay on)
- Wipes or some other way to clean the clay off their hands
- Snacks
- Figure 35 Note to parents

Teacher prep: Please read the Scriptures taught in today's lesson at least a couple of times. The more we understand them, the better we can explain them to the children. Pray for the children, for the class, for your abilities as a loving and effective teacher, and for understanding. (As the Word says, pastors and teachers are held to a higher standard.)

- ❖ The lure

Music: "Wide, Wide Is the Ocean," (Cedarmont Kids, 100 Singalong Bible Songs for Kids, vol. 3 #7); "I'm Gonna Sing, Sing, Sing," (Cedarmont Kids, Bible Singalong Collection 2)

Review of previous lesson(s)

Bible review: *What is the Bible?* (God's letter to us)
How many main sections are there in the Bible? (two)
What are they called? (the Old Testament and the New Testament)
Do you remember what a "testament" is? (a covenant or an agreement)
What is the first book in the Bible? (Genesis)
What does "Genesis" mean? (Beginnings)
Do we find Genesis in the Old Testament or the New Testament? (Old Testament)
Can you find Genesis?
What is the last book in the Bible? (Revelation)
Can you find Revelation?

- ❖ The cast

Pass out sheets of wax paper (about 12"X12") and modeling clay.
Ask the children to make a person out of the clay. (Kids often like it when the teacher participates in the crafts, too.) When they have finished, they can set their little characters aside and wash their hands. (Allow about 5 minutes for this craft.)

As you are passing out the Bibles, explain that in this lesson we're going to learn how God created people. (Notice that in verse 26 of chapter 1, God says, "*Let us make man in our image.*" He did not say, "Let us make "a" man;" He said "man". I interpret this to mean "mankind." He may well have made others after He made Adam and Eve. Otherwise, who would their children marry? It's also possible that, although the Bible names only three of Adam's children, they could have produced several more, both boys and girls, in which case siblings could have married each other. The Bible isn't clear about this, but these are two possibilities.)

Ask them to find Genesis (which means?), Chapter 2: verse 2 and to put their fingers on the verse when they've located it.

Read to them or ask them to take turns reading the scripture passage for the lesson, stopping to clarify or explain as you go along.

> *By the seventh day God had finished the work he had been doing, so on the seventh day he rested from all his work. (V. 3) And God blessed the seventh day and made it holy, because on it he rested from all the work of creating that he had done.*

Now let's look at verses 4-6.

> *When the Lord God made the earth and the heavens—* (5) *and no shrub of the field had yet appeared and no plant of the field had yet sprung up, for the Lord God had not sent rain on the earth, and there was no man to work the ground,* (6) *but streams came up from the earth and watered the whole surface of the ground—*

Wow! What did that say? It said that no plants had come up in the fields. That meant that no beans or corn or wheat, or anything that farmers plant for food had come up. Why do you suppose He hadn't made these kinds of plants yet? It was because there weren't any people yet to work the ground, plant the seed, or harvest the crops yet. (v.5)

Another interesting thought is that God hadn't yet sent rain to water the earth. So, how did the trees and shrubs and flowers and grasses get the water they *needed to live? Look at verse 6..."but streams came up from the earth (ground) and watered the whole surface of the ground."*

This is important, and we'll talk more about this in a later lesson.

Now, to the exciting part...Let's read verse 7 together.

> **"The Lord God formed the man from the dust of the ground and breathed into his nostrils the breath of life, and the man became a living being."**

There are a couple of really cool things to notice in this verse...We made our little characters out of clay. But are they alive? Can they speak or move or get up and walk around or even breathe? Why? (because they aren't alive.)

What did God make man out of? Did He just speak the words, "Let there be" like He did when He created the sun and moon? No, He reached down and got a handful of dirt and made a man….just as he is, with heads and arms and legs and stomachs and backs and fingers and toes and all the things inside of them that made them "work"...all the parts that go into the making of a person.

Another really cool thing to know is that in the Hebrew language (that's what God's chosen people are called...Hebrews...and their language is called Hebrew...just like the language we speak is called English)... the word for "dirt" is <u>adamah</u>. (If you have a dry erase board, it would be good to write the word, "adamah" on the board so they can notice the spelling.) *Can you find the name "Adam" in the word "<u>adamah</u>"?*

Now, after He formed the man out of dirt, the man was kind of like your little clay people; he wasn't alive yet. What do animals have to be able to do to be alive? (breathe) *That's right. If they can't breathe, they can't live. So, what did God do about that?* (He breathed into man's nostrils.)

That's exciting!!! Man became a living being because he had the very breath of the Almighty God in him. Can you see how God is making a person in His own image?...by giving the man His own breath!

Okay...now we have a living, breathing person here. He needs a place to live. So, let's read on and see what God did about that. Look at verses 8 & 9, and let's read.

> *"Now the Lord God had planted a garden in the east, in Eden; and there he put the man he had formed. (v. 9) And the Lord God made all kinds of trees grow out of the ground—trees that were pleasing to the eye and good for food. In the middle of the garden were the tree of life and the tree of the knowledge of good and evil."*

Let's stop there for just a minute. What did God do with the first man, Adam? (Put him in a garden made just for him.) *According to what we just read, God had already prepared the garden for the man. What does that tell us about God? Did He have a plan? Was he taking good care of the man he had made? Or did he just dump him down in the middle of nowhere and say, "You're on your own, kid. Good luck!"? Of course not. Why do you think He wanted to make sure the man had everything he needed?* ***(because He <u>loved</u> him.)***

(Let's skip verses 10-14 for now. It deals with the rivers that flow from the Garden of Eden and isn't a vital part of the lesson.)

Let's see what God did next, after He breathed His own breath into Adam and set him down into a beautiful garden. Skip down to verses 15 & 16.

> *"The Lord God took the man and put him in the Garden of Eden to work it and take care of it."*

God put the man in a place created especially for him and gave him a job to do. He gave the man only one law:

> v. 16 *And the Lord God commanded the man, "You are free to eat from any tree in the garden; but you must not eat from the tree of the knowledge of good and evil, for when you eat of it, you will surely die."*

Uh-oh! God gave the man only one rule, or commandment...what was it? (Not to eat fruit from the tree of the knowledge of good and evil) *And what would happen to the man if he did eat the fruit from that tree?* (He would die.)

Do any of you have younger brothers or sisters or cousins? When they are maybe two or three years old, old enough to get into things and do things that they shouldn't do, do they always know they shouldn't do those things? No, of course not. They're just babies. They have to be taught that some things are good to do and some things are not. God doesn't consider very small children to be sinning when they misbehave because they don't know any better.

Sometimes we have to be taught that if we do certain things, we will be punished. And that's the way it is with children until they get old enough to understand that, not only will they be punished for doing certain things, but that there are things that are actually wrong. And there are some things that are right. Usually children are about 12 years old before they can understand this idea. Then they are old enough to know the difference between right and wrong, good and evil.

So, when God first placed Adam in the garden, he didn't know anything about good and evil. He was, in this way, like a small child. Now, let's look in our Bibles and find verse 18.

> *v. 18 The Lord God said, "It is not good for man to be alone. I will make a helper suitable for him."*
>
> *Vs. 19-22...Now the Lord God had formed out of the ground all the beasts of the field and all the birds of the air. He brought them to the man to see what he would name them; and whatever the man called each living creature, that was its name.*
>
> *v. 20 So the man gave names to all the livestock, the birds of the air and all the beasts of the field. But for Adam no suitable helper was found. (v. 21) So the Lord God caused the man to fall into a deep sleep; and while he was sleeping, he took one of the man's ribs and closed up the place with flesh. (v. 22) Then the Lord God made a woman from the rib he had taken out of the man, and he brought her to the man.*

Here we find God once more loving the man He had made and taking care of him. Adam was lonely with just the animals and no one to talk to that would understand him, and no one to help him take care of the garden. So God gave him a partner.

- The catch  Color page (figure 34) Children can eat while they color.

- The feast

Figure 34

Figure 35 Note to parents, Lesson 7

Thank you for sharing your child with us today. We learned about how God created Adam, and later, how and why He created Eve…and about how Adam was given the joy of naming each animal. Genesis 1:27; Genesis 2: 4-8, 15-22

Thank you for sharing your child with us today. We learned about how God created Adam, and later, how and why He created Eve…and about how Adam was given the joy of naming each animal. Genesis 1:27; Genesis 2: 4-8, 15-22

Thank you for sharing your child with us today. We learned about how God created Adam, and later, how and why He created Eve…and about how Adam was given the joy of naming each animal. Genesis 1:27; Genesis 2: 4-8, 15-22

Thank you for sharing your child with us today. We learned about how God created Adam, and later, how and why He created Eve…and about how Adam was given the joy of naming each animal. Genesis 1:27; Genesis 2: 4-8, 15-22

Thank you for sharing your child with us today. We learned about how God created Adam, and later, how and why He created Eve…and about how Adam was given the joy of naming each animal. Genesis 1:27; Genesis 2: 4-8, 15-22

Thank you for sharing your child with us today. We learned about how God created Adam, and later, how and why He created Eve…and about how Adam was given the joy of naming each animal. Genesis 1:27; Genesis 2: 4-8, 15-22

Thank you for sharing your child with us today. We learned about how God created Adam, and later, how and why He created Eve…and about how Adam was given the joy of naming each animal. Genesis 1:27; Genesis 2: 4-8, 15-22

LET'S GO FISHING, LESSON 8
The Creation of Eve & the Fall of Man

For your spirit…Please Read

> The fact that God is light sets up a natural contrast with darkness. If light is a metaphor for righteousness and goodness, then darkness signifies evil and sin. First John 1:6 says that "if we claim to have fellowship with him and yet walk in the darkness, we lie and do not live out the truth." Verse 5 says, "God is light; in him there is no darkness at all." Note that we are not told that God is a light but that He is light. Light is part of His essence, as is love (1 John 4:8). The message is that God is completely, unreservedly, absolutely holy, with no admixture of sin, no taint of iniquity, and no hint of injustice.
>
> God is light, and it is His plan that believers shine forth His light, becoming more like Christ every day. "You are all children of the light and children of the day. We do not belong to the night or to the darkness" (1 Thessalonians 5:5). God is the Creator of physical light as well as the Giver of spiritual light by which we can see the truth. Light exposes that which is hidden in darkness; it shows things as they really are. To walk in the light means to know God, understand the truth, and live in righteousness.

Scripture Reference: Genesis 2: 23-25, all of Chapter 3, Revelation 13:8(b)

Memory Verse: **God is light, and in him is no darkness at all.** 1 John 1:5

Emphasis: Adam and Eve had it made! God had provided them with everything they needed to be safe, well-fed and happy. But they disobeyed and brought sin into the world.

Supplies needed:
- A Bible for each child
- Music "The Boss of Me" by Crossroad Kids (There is a good YouTube post called "God is Light" that you might want to listen to or share with your students sung by Lisa Cochran.); "This Little Light of Mine," Cedarmont Kids Singalong Bible Songs CD, Vol.2
- If you can get a pair of blackout blindfolds (the kind people wear to block out all light so they can sleep), they will come in handy in this lesson. If not, you can rig up a blindfold that will allow no light to come through.

86

> ➢ Snacks
> ➢ Crayons, colored pencils, or fine-tip markers
> ➢ Copy of the coloring page for each child
> ➢ Copy of the note to parents for each child

Teacher prep: This is a very important lesson, one in which you can help the children understand what sin is, how it came into the world, and the consequences of sin. This is a deep concept, but, with your help, they should be able to begin to grasp it. And these events put into motion God's master Plan to bring His children back to him. Revelation 13: 8(b) refers to *the Lamb that was slain from the creation of the world*. So God knew from the very beginning that His only Son would have to pay the price for the sins of mankind and conquer the sin nature that dwells in each of us. The children need to know exactly what sin is...rebellion and disobedience toward God. You might want to stress that He's the boss. He made us and He has the right to tell us what to do.

Welcome: Try to make sure every child feels welcome and valued. Often their first glimpse of Jesus is what they see in us. Have the Bibles on the chairs or tables

❖ The lure

> ➢ Music: "The Boss of Me"; "This Little Light of Mine," Cedarmont Kids Singalong Bible Songs CD, Vol.2

❖ The cast

If you remember, we've been talking about how God created the earth and the whole universe. Does anyone remember the very first thing God did when He looked down on the dark shapeless blob that would eventually become our planet? (He said, "Let there be light.") *So, the very first thing He did was to introduce, or insert, light into the darkness. Did you ever wonder why?* (Allow time for several responses. Sometimes kids can surprise us with their understanding.)

Let's conduct a little experiment. Who would like to help me? You'll have to wear a blindfold, so don't volunteer if that frightens you. Don't worry, we're not going to do anything that will hurt or scare you.

When you have your volunteer, secure the blindfold to completely cover your volunteer's eyes. Then ask...

Can you see anything? Anything at all? Why not? This is what people who are blind see. Nothing...nothing but darkness. Would you want to have to go around all day long and do the things you need to do or want to do in complete darkness? Why? (possible answers: you might bump into something; you might fall off something and hurt or kill yourself; you couldn't see where you were going; you might step in front of a car or train; etc.)

Ask the masked student to stand up. Place him/her somewhere in the room as far away from other people or objects as possible. Then tell him that if he will do exactly what you say to do, he won't get hurt.
Direct him to a wall or table, etc. by telling him to go straight ahead or right or left until he gets there. When he reaches the destination, remove the mask.
Ask: *Why was it important to do exactly what I said?* (Because if he/she didn't, that child might bump into something or someone.)

Do you think people who want to hurt someone or steal something would like the dark? Why? (They wouldn't want others to see what they were doing.)

Our memory verse today talks about that very thing. It's short and easy. Let's learn it right now before we get on with our Bible story.

"God is light, and in him there is no darkness at all." 1 John 1:5

In the Bible, light represents goodness, and darkness represents bad things like sin and evil. We've learned that God is totally light with no darkness creeping in around the edges. He is completely good, holy, and pure. Light is part of his essence, part of who He is. It is His nature. He cannot be sinful or mean or stingy or unfaithful any more than we, people, can be something that is contrary to who we are-- like dogs or houses or trees.

But there's someone else who is just the opposite of God...His enemy, the devil, whose name is Satan. He is totally darkness and evil. He's always trying to mess up what God has made to be good. God placed Adam and Eve in a garden, in a world where everything He had made, everything He saw, was good.

When God put Adam and Eve in the Garden of _____?, they were like Him in that they were innocent and good. They couldn't do anything wrong because there was no sin, because they didn't know right from wrong, except that they knew they should obey God. And they did just that... in the beginning.

Give them a brief review of the creation of Adam and Eve.

Let's turn in our Bibles to the 3rd chapter of Genesis and find verse 1.
> Now the serpent was more crafty than any of the wild animals the Lord God had made.

Sometimes we think of a crafty person as someone who likes to make cool things out of clay or wood or paper, etc. But In this verse "crafty" means sneaky or clever or deceitful. And the serpent was Satan in disguise. (Revelation 12:9 refers to "the ancient serpent, called the devil, or Satan.)
And we know from what happens a little later on that he probably had legs, more like a lizard than a snake. He was also probably very beautiful. If sin and Satan looked ugly, very few people would be interested in him or in doing what is wrong. And he wanted to trick Eve into disobeying God, so he wanted to look like something pleasant so she would trust him and not be afraid of him.

So, here we have Adam and Eve, "tooling" along and having a great time in the Garden, talking, singing, laughing, and taking care of the garden. Any time they got tired, they rested, and any time they got hungry, they just reached up and pulled a piece of fruit, an apple, orange, pear, or banana off a tree. They probably had olives and avocados and all kinds of berries, too.

They may have played with the animals or played hide-and-seek with each other. They might have even made up songs to sing. Sounds like a pretty good life, huh? But Satan can't stand to see us obeying God or being happy. He hates God, and so he hates the ones God loves...and that was Adam and Eve, and it's also us.

Now the serpent enters the scene. He wants to mess things up for Adam and Eve. Let's listen to what the serpent said to Eve when he came to her in the Garden...
> *He said to the woman, "Did God **really** say, 'You must not eat from any tree in the garden'?"*

Oops! IS that what God told Adam and Eve? Did you notice how the serpent took what God said and twisted it so that it didn't say what God meant at all?

Let's read the 2nd verse..."The woman said to the serpent, "We may eat fruit from the trees in the garden, but God did say, 'You must not eat fruit from the tree that is in the middle of the garden, and you must not touch it, or you will die.'"
(We're paraphrasing the rest of the story for the sake of time.)

But the serpent told Eve that they would not die...that God didn't want them to eat the fruit from that tree because He knew that if they did, they would be like Him! Here Satan is calling God a liar. Now, God is perfect, and He NEVER lies!

Eve must have smiled as she thought, "Wow! Wouldn't it be great to be LIKE GOD???" And when she looked and saw that the fruit was beautiful and looked so delicious, and thought that eating it would make her wise like God, she reached up and plucked one of them off the tree.
But when lightning didn't strike and she didn't fall down dead the moment she touched it, she took a chance, and took a bite. The fruit from the tree of the knowledge of good and evil was delicious, and, since she didn't die, she offered some to Adam who was with her at the time. Adam said, "OK", and he ate some of it, too…………………

And nothing happened, at least nothing that they could see. But Adam and Eve may have looked the same, and may have even felt the same, but there was a difference deep down inside, where it counts. Before they decided to disobey God, they were innocent. Now, they knew the difference between things that were good and things that were bad, between what was right and what was wrong. And they also noticed that they were naked and were ashamed.

Have you ever been ashamed...for something you did that was wrong, or because you said something that hurt someone or embarrassed you?

Before what is called "The Fall"...that's when Adam and Eve disobeyed God... they were like children. But now things were different. They knew that certain parts of their bodies were private.

They gathered some leaves from a fig tree and sewed them together to cover up those parts that shouldn't be seen in public. They weren't happy anymore. They became worried and scared.

And now comes the really sad part. God loved to walk and talk with Adam and Eve in the Garden. Like all good fathers, He loved them and loved spending time with them. Later in that same day, in the cool of the evening, God came walking in the Garden. He called Adam, but Adam didn't answer. He and Eve had hidden themselves from God. They felt guilty. Why do you suppose they felt guilty? What had they done that God told them specifically that they shouldn't do? Would God know what they had done without seeing them or without them telling Him about it? What do you think?

God asked Adam where he was. Do you think God knew all along where Adam was? Of course, He did. But He called out to Adam, anyway. He wanted Adam to answer Him and to own up to the fact that he had disobeyed God.

Let's find verse 10 and see how Adam answered when God called him.
> "I heard you in the garden, and I was afraid because I was naked, so I hid." (v.11) And he (God) said, 'Who told you that you were naked? Have you eaten from the tree that I commanded you not to eat from?'"

Look at how Adam answered God in v. 12...
> The man said, "The women you put here with me—she gave me some fruit from the tree, and I ate it."

What? What did Adam just do? Did he take responsibility and confess his disobedience? Or did he try to blame someone else? Whom did he blame? (first Eve, and then God.) *He said "the woman" that YOU gave me"...*
First he blamed Eve for giving him the fruit, and then he blamed God for putting Eve in the garden with him. Oops!

Do we ever try to do that when we've done something we shouldn't have...put the blame on someone or something else?

Let's read the next verse and see what God said to Eve...
> Then the Lord God said to the woman, "What is this you have done?" The woman said, "The serpent deceived me, and I ate."

Was she telling the truth? Did the serpent trick her? How? (By suggesting that God was lying to her, that He really just didn't want her and Adam to be as smart as He was; and by implying that eating fruit from the tree of knowledge of good and evil would make her as wise as God was.)

This is the deal...God didn't want them to know the difference between right and wrong because if they did, they would always have to choose which way to go...to obey or not to obey, to be kind or to be cruel, to be honest or to be dishonest. If we don't know what is right and wrong, then we don't sin...just like a little child. If he wants something that someone else has, he takes it; if he wants to play in the street, he tries to do it; if he wants to put his hand into the fire, he reaches for it; if he wants to eat half a bag of cookies, he tries to do it; if he gets angry or doesn't get his way, he often hits or bites or screams. And each one of these actions, and a lot of others, hurt either him or someone else. They are wrong, but a small child doesn't know right from wrong.

That's why God gives us several years to teach children what they should and shouldn't do.

Adam and Eve didn't know, either, when God first put them in the garden. But after they ate the fruit from the Tree, their spiritual eyes were opened, and they knew. And once they knew, they were held accountable for their actions.

- ❖ The catch

Coloring page: "The serpent in the garden" This page will probably take some time depending on the ages of your students.

The feast　　　　Snacks

Figure 36

Figure 37: Note to parents

Dear Parents: Today we learned a very important lesson, about how Adam and Eve listened to the serpent instead of obeying God and how their decisions affected them and the rest of mankind. The memory verse was: "God is light, and in him there is no darkness at all." 1 John 1:5

Dear Parents: Today we learned a very important lesson, about how Adam and Eve listened to the serpent instead of obeying God and how their decisions affected them and the rest of mankind. The memory verse was: "God is light, and in him there is no darkness at all." 1 John 1:5

Dear Parents: Today we learned a very important lesson, about how Adam and Eve listened to the serpent instead of obeying God and how their decisions affected them and the rest of mankind. The memory verse was: "God is light, and in him there is no darkness at all." 1 John 1:5

Dear Parents: Today we learned a very important lesson, about how Adam and Eve listened to the serpent instead of obeying God and how their decisions affected them and the rest of mankind. The memory verse was: "God is light, and in him there is no darkness at all." 1 John 1:5

Dear Parents: Today we learned a very important lesson, about how Adam and Eve listened to the serpent instead of obeying God and how their decisions affected them and the rest of mankind. The memory verse was: "God is light, and in him there is no darkness at all." 1 John 1:5

Dear Parents: Today we learned a very important lesson, about how Adam and Eve listened to the serpent instead of obeying God and how their decisions affected them and the rest of mankind. The memory verse was: "God is light, and in him there is no darkness at all." 1 John 1:5

Dear Parents: Today we learned a very important lesson, about how Adam and Eve listened to the serpent instead of obeying God and how their decisions affected them and the rest of mankind. The memory verse was: "God is light, and in him there is no darkness at all." 1 John 1:5

LET'S GO FISHING, LESSON 9
Adam and Eve Expelled from the Garden

For your spirit:

> Speaking to the serpent, God declared, "I will put enmity between you and the woman, and between your offspring and her offspring; he shall crush your head, and you shall bruise his heel." (Gen 3:15). We don't get any more information than this for now. But what we do have is a promise that someone is coming, a descendent of the woman, who will destroy the tempting serpent by crushing his head, and the sin and evil associated with it. And, with this promise, God declares that he has not given up on his plan. The suggestion is that one day things will again be the way that they were supposed to be. One day….(A discourse by Western Seminary)

Scripture reference: Genesis 3:20-24

Memory verse: "**For the wages of sin is death, but the gift of God is eternal life in Christ Jesus our Lord**." Romans 6:23

Emphasis: The sin of Adam and Eve caused a separation between God and his creation. But in Christ, He made a way for that fellowship to be restored.

Supplies needed:
- A Bible for each child
- Crayons or water colors. (water, paints, paper towels, brushes needed for watercolor)
- A copy of figure 38 (color page) for each child
- A copy of note to parent, figure 39
- Music…your choice; children's favorites from any of the CD's mentioned
- Snacks…suggestion: fruit (as if from the Garden of Eden)

Teacher prep: Read the scripture passage several times, including the ones from the previous lesson so that you are completely familiar with the events, and the significance of them, in the passages.

Welcome:

❖ The lure

Music: Your choice

Review of previous lesson and memory verse

Today's memory verse: *"For the wages of sin is death, but the gift of God is eternal life in Christ Jesus our Lord."* Romans 6:23
    Repeat, one phrase at a time, until the children know it well.

❖ The cast

Before Adam and Eve disobeyed God, all they had known in their lives were blessings. They had a wonderful place to live, a worthwhile job to do, good companions, all the food they could ever want, and the beauty of God's creation all around them. They could also walk and talk with God, their Creator and could delight in that fellowship.

But when the serpent, the devil, lied to them and tempted them to disobey God, each one of them had a choice...they could choose to obey the kind, loving God who created them, or they could decide they wanted something else, something out of God's will for their lives. They wanted to be like God. In essence, they wanted to be their own gods, to make their own decisions, to have their own way, to do what they wanted to, instead of trusting God to know what was best for them.

What did God say would happen if they ate from the tree of the knowledge of good and evil? **(They would die.)** *But did they die right then? No, but with their disobedience, sin and death were introduced into the Garden and into the perfect world God had made.*

When we disobey our parents or teachers or the law, what can we expect to happen? (Allow for several answers; this could be an eye-opener. Always listen for anything that "smacks" of child abuse in their answers.) *Do people get rewarded for doing the wrong thing? Do your parents say, "OK...good job!" when you've disobeyed them? Well, God didn't reward Adam and Eve, either. Although they didn't die immediately, death did come to the garden that same day. Let's open our Bibles and find Genesis, chapter 3, verse 14.*

> *So the Lord God said to the serpent, "Because you have done this, cursed are you above all the livestock and all the wild animals. You will crawl on your belly and you will eat dust all the days of your life."*

Notice what God said. He said, "cursed are you." Before this time, God's creation had known only blessings. But now God has put a curse on the serpent. Who knows what it means to put a curse on someone? This verse doesn't mean to use ugly words. When God says it, it means that He will use His supernatural powers to punish or harm someone. A curse is the exact opposite of a blessing.

So, now, because of what he had done, the serpent will have to crawl on his belly and eat dust. This would seem to imply that before this curse, he had legs. Isn't that what it sounds like to you?

Let's read verse 15 to see what else God said would happen to the serpent (the devil).

> *"And I will put enmity between you and the woman, and between your offspring and hers; he will crush your head, and you will strike his heal."*

"Enmity" is a word we don't use very often. It means hatred and war. So, God is saying that there would always be war between Satan and women and their children. That's interesting, isn't it? It doesn't say that there would always be a war between men and Satan. Why do you suppose that is?

Do you think maybe that is because Satan tricked Eve into disobeying God, and she, and all other women who are born after her, will be angry with him for doing it?

Look at the injuries that would occur between the children (or Child) of women, or a woman, (Mary), and Satan. Satan will strike the Child's heel, but the Child will crush Satan's head. Which injury is more likely to be deadly...hurting someone's foot or crushing his head? In this verse is a promise that someday, the offspring of a woman (Jesus) would destroy Satan and his power over people.

(Allow time for children to express their thoughts.)

Now, let's see what punishment would come to Eve (and to all women in the future) because of her disobedience. Find verse 16…

> To the woman he said, "I will greatly increase your pains in childbearing; with pain you will give birth to children. Your desire will be for your husband, and he will rule over you."

And what punishment did Adam receive? Let's read the verses 17-19…

> (v. 17) To Adam he said, "Because you listened to your wife and ate from the tree about which I commanded you, 'You must not eat of it, '<u>cursed is the ground</u> because of you; through painful toil you will eat of it all the days of your life. (v. 18) It will produce thorns and thistles for you, and you will eat the plants of the field. (V. 19) By the sweat of your brow you will eat your food until you return to the ground, since from it you were taken; for dust you are and to dust you will return."

Up until Adam and Eve disobeyed God, what has the ground produced? (fruit trees, berries, etc., so that all Adam and Eve had to do when they were hungry was to reach up and grab something to eat.) *But now, things have changed. The ground isn't going to produce all the food Adam and Eve would need. What did it say in verse 18?* (That the ground would now produce thorns and thistles…in other word weeds that hurt and make it difficult to grow grains and vegetables and fruit!)

And how will Adam be able to provide food for himself and Eve and any children they would have? (He would have to work hard for it.)
Adam and Eve didn't die the moment they ate the forbidden fruit, but God promised them that eventually, they would die because sin brings death. And what would happen to their bodies when they died? (They would return to the ground because before God got hold of the soil and made people, that's all they were…just a handful of dirt!)

Verse 20 tells us that Adam named his wife, "Eve", because she would become the mother of all people. (The word "eve" sounds like the Hebrew word for "living".) *But verse 21 tells us about another result of their sin (disobedience). Except for a few fig leaves sewn together, Adam and Eve were still mostly naked. God is the great problem-solver, but how He solved the problem of clothes for them is another result of their sin.*

They didn't have cloth to make clothes, and there was nothing to make cloth out of. So, do you know what God had to do? He had to kill an animal, or animals, (the Bible doesn't say what kind of animal) and use the skin to make coverings for them. So, really, death did come to the Garden that day. Adam and Eve didn't die immediately, but one or more of God's other creatures did.

Do you think it made them sad to see one of the animals they loved die because of what they had done?

If you remember, God put another tree in the center of the Garden of Eden. Do you remember what it was? (the Tree of Life). *If they ate from that tree, they would live forever. Now, that might sound good, but Adam and Eve had already proved that sometimes they weren't obedient, nor did they always make wise decisions. They had become sinful, and as sinful people they could never live in Heaven with God. Only those who have been redeemed (saved) and died can enter the Kingdom of Heaven.*

So, God had to make them leave the Garden of Eden, and to make sure that they couldn't come back and eat fruit from the Tree of Life and live forever as sinful people, he placed cherubim and a flaming sword to keep them out forever.

Baptisttabernacleonline.com

BibelSvar

Do you see what sin did? How it hurt God? How it hurt Adam and Eve? Sin ALWAYS hurts; even though sometimes we can't see the pain, it is the natural consequence of sin.

The catch

Color page**, figure 38**

- ❖ The feast

Snacks

Figure 38

Figure 39

Today's lesson was a very important one. It deals with sin and its consequences. You might want to ask your child about this…what the first sin was, what happened to Adam and Eve after they sinned. Emphasis: Sin always hurts and always has consequences. Memory verse: *"For the wages of sin is death, but the gift of God is eternal life in Christ Jesus our Lord."* Romans 6:23

Today's lesson was a very important one. It deals with sin and its consequences. You might want to ask your child about this…what the first sin was, what happened to Adam and Eve after they sinned. Emphasis: Sin always hurts and always has consequences. Memory verse: *"For the wages of sin is death, but the gift of God is eternal life in Christ Jesus our Lord."* Romans 6:23

Today's lesson was a very important one. It deals with sin and its consequences. You might want to ask your child about this…what the first sin was, what happened to Adam and Eve after they sinned. Emphasis: Sin always hurts and always has consequences. Memory verse: *"For the wages of sin is death, but the gift of God is eternal life in Christ Jesus our Lord."* Romans 6:23

Today's lesson was a very important one. It deals with sin and its consequences. You might want to ask your child about this…what the first sin was, what happened to Adam and Eve after they sinned. Emphasis: Sin always hurts and always has consequences. Memory verse: *"For the wages of sin is death, but the gift of God is eternal life in Christ Jesus our Lord."* Romans 6:23

Today's lesson was a very important one. It deals with sin and its consequences. You might want to ask your child about this…what the first sin was, what happened to Adam and Eve after they sinned. Emphasis: Sin always hurts and always has consequences. Memory verse: *"For the wages of sin is death, but the gift of God is eternal life in Christ Jesus our Lord."* Romans 6:23

LET'S GO FISHING, LESSON 10
Review and Bible Games

For your spirit:

> The call to teach children is one of the highest and most important callings there is. It means doing more than just entertaining them or keeping them busy while their parents are not with them. We have the opportunity to introduce them to the infallible truths of the Word. The lessons, scriptures and songs they learn will stay with them for a lifetime. May God richly bless your life and your spirit as you continue on this journey.

Supplies needed:

- Bible Memory matching pages, figures #40 & 41
- Bible for each student
- Music: "Down in My Heart," Cedarmont Kids; "Every Time I Feel the Spirit," Cedarmont Kids; or "The B-I-B-L-E," Cedarmont Kids.
- Copies of Creation activity page, figure 42
- Copies of Note to parents, figure 43
- A pencil for each child

Teacher prep: Always... prayers for yourself and your students. Make copies of the memory matching game on plain paper or white or colored card stock. Cut each copied page horizontally, then separate the individual verses by cutting on the dotted lines with paper cutter, scissors or craft scissors.
You'll need knowledge of Bible Drill procedures.

❖ The lure

Music: (see above)

❖ The cast

Review the memory verses from the past lessons before gathering your students into groups to play the Memory Verse Matching game.

To play the game, shuffle all the verse beginnings and place them on the left side of the table and all the verse endings on the right. You may either let each child have a turn matching one pair, or, if you have enough for more than one team, make matching the verse pairs a competition, seeing which team can match all the verses first.

After the game, pass out the Bibles, one per child. Review these facts by asking these questions…

How many main parts are there in the Bible? (two)
Who remembers what they are? (the old testament and the new testament)
What does the word "testament" mean? (an agreement or covenant)
What is the first book in the Bible? (Genesis)
Who remembers what Genesis means? (beginnings)
Let's see who can find Genesis in the Bible…
What is the last book in the Bible? (Revelation)
Can you find the book of Revelation in your Bible?
Let's play a little game called "Bible Drill". Everyone stand against the wall (or on a line) facing me. (If you've never participated in a Bible drill, you'll need to do a little research on this procedure.)
Can you remember the first four books in the Bible? (Genesis, Exodus, Leviticus, Numbers)

When I say "Attention!" hold your Bible in your right hand at your side with your fingers touching the front of the Bible. (It is suggested that a driller who searches with his <u>right hand</u> should hold the Bible in his left hand with Genesis down and the right hand resting flat on top of the Bible. A driller who searches with his <u>left hand</u> should hold the Bible in his right hand, Genesis up, with left hand resting flat on the front cover of the Bible. There are some videos online if you want to explore them.)

The Bible says that the Word of God, which is the Bible, is sharper than any two-edged sword, so when I say draw your swords, bring your Bible, your sword, forward and place it on the palm of your open left hand of you with your right hand holding your "sword" and your left hand on top. I'll tell you what book of the Bible you need to find. And then, when I say begin, you find the book in your Bible as quickly as you can. When you've found it, place a finger on a page in that book and take one step forward.

Ask them to find Genesis first. When all students have found it and stepped forward, you will say "attention" again, and they will return to their original places. Then go through the same procedure and ask them to find Revelation. Kids usually love this little competition.

The book that comes right after Genesis is Exodus. Can you find it?

When they can find Exodus, move on to Leviticus, and then Numbers. This is more challenging and will take more practice, but it's a good start in helping them be able to find the books they are looking for.

You can repeat this little exercise several times until the students are pretty secure in their knowledge of where these books are.

After they can find these five books easily, you can show them how to find Isaiah. Hold the Bible in front of you vertically, spine edge down, page edges up. Ask them to put their thumbnails as close to the middle of the Bible as they can and open it. Most of them will open to a chapter in Isaiah. This will differ with some Bibles because of variables such as maps, indexes, etc, but it's a good exercise. Then, if they take only the second half of their Bibles and divide that in half, they should open to Matthew or close to it. Take them as far as you feel they are comfortable with. It's best to not propose so much that it frustrates or discourages them.

❖ The catch

Figure 42 Creation Activity page

❖ The feast

Snacks:

Figure 40

****

God is Spirit, and his worshipers	must worship in spirit and in truth. John 4:24

****

In the beginning, God created	the heavens and the earth. Genesis 1:1

****

The heavens declare	the glory of God. Psalm 19:1

****

For nothing is impossible	with God. Luke 1:37

****

The word of God is living and active	and sharper than any two-edged sword. Hebrews 4:12

Figure 41

In the beginning was the Word, and the Word was WITH God and the Word WAS God. John 1:1

****

Blessed are those who hear the word of God and obey it. Luke 11:28

****

God is light, and in him is no darkness at all. 1 John 1:5

****

For the wages of sin is Death, but the gift of God is eternal life In Jesus Christ, our Lord. Romans 6:23

****

Figure 42

Creation Activity Worksheet
by SundaySchoolResources.co.uk

Across

2 God created the moon on this day (6)
4 The earth was this before the creation (5)
5 God created these on the 5th day (5)
7 God created these on the 3rd day (5)
9 The name of the Garden the man and woman lived in (4)
10 God created this on the 1st day (5)

Down

1 The name of the man that God created (4)
3 God did this on the 7th day (6)
4 The name of the woman that God created (3)
6 God created the woman by taking this from the man (3)
8 God created land creatures on this day (5)

ANIMALS
BEGINNING
CREATION
EARTH
GARDEN
GOD
HEAVENS
LIGHT
MAN
PLANTS
SEA
STARS
WOMAN

F	H	R	A	U	N	W	B	V	N	R	F	E
P	V	N	N	U	C	R	E	A	T	I	O	N
M	U	A	I	Y	G	W	G	V	N	Y	S	C
L	E	M	M	Q	W	Q	I	K	W	W	T	N
S	T	D	A	E	K	M	N	L	A	T	N	E
U	P	J	L	O	T	M	N	V	Y	X	A	D
K	N	Q	S	G	O	D	I	S	I	X	L	R
H	A	H	E	A	V	E	N	S	T	H	P	A
H	M	B	E	F	G	S	G	S	W	A	X	G
Y	O	G	M	A	K	Q	L	N	T	W	R	Y
Y	W	T	W	S	R	T	H	G	I	L	C	S
M	P	M	K	F	Z	T	H	B	C	B	C	H
J	L	P	X	I	K	C	H	S	O	U	C	F

Note to parents figure 43

Dear Parents, today we reviewed all the Bible memory verses we've learned and played a memory verse matching game. We also had a Bible drill, finding the first and last books of the Bible before we worked on a Creation Story worksheet.

Dear Parents, today we reviewed all the Bible memory verses we've learned and played a memory verse matching game. We also had a Bible drill, finding the first and last books of the Bible before we worked on a Creation Story worksheet.

Dear Parents, today we reviewed all the Bible memory verses we've learned and played a memory verse matching game. We also had a Bible drill, finding the first and last books of the Bible before we worked on a Creation Story worksheet.

Dear Parents, today we reviewed all the Bible memory verses we've learned and played a memory verse matching game. We also had a Bible drill, finding the first and last books of the Bible before we worked on a Creation Story worksheet.

Dear Parents, today we reviewed all the Bible memory verses we've learned and played a memory verse matching game. We also had a Bible drill, finding the first and last books of the Bible before we worked on a Creation Story worksheet.

Dear Parents, today we reviewed all the Bible memory verses we've learned and played a memory verse matching game. We also had a Bible drill, finding the first and last books of the Bible before we worked on a Creation Story worksheet.

Dear Parents, today we reviewed all the Bible memory verses we've learned and played a memory verse matching game. We also had a Bible drill, finding the first and last books of the Bible before we worked on a Creation Story worksheet.

LET'S GO FISHING, LESSON 11
Noah Builds the Ark

For your spirit:

> The test of a person's character is not what he/she does in the exceptional moments of life, but what he does in the ordinary, everyday times. God sees us when we are "nobody" doing nothing noteworthy or spectacular. That's when character tells. It's often the decisions we make and the things we do and the way we do them when no one is watching that determine who we are and Whose we are. The children we reach through teaching God's Word may have a much more powerful effect on the world than we will ever know. God bless.

Scripture reference: Genesis 6, 7 & 8

Memory verse: ***There is a way that seems right to man, but in the end, it leads to death.*** Proverbs 16:23

Emphasis: When people turn their backs on God and disobey everything He tells them, He eventually puts an end to their rebellion. But He rewards those who love, serve and obey Him.

Supplies needed:
- Bible for each child
- Dark-colored crayons for each child (black, dark blue, dark brown, dark purple)
- Scissors for each child
- Dark-colored plastic tape (1" width)
- Cardstock or copy paper
- A copy of the ark template for each child
- A tray and water to provide the "lake" for the boats to float in
- Animal crackers for snack???
- A copy of the note to parents for each child

Teacher prep: Make copies of ark template (**figure 45**) on cardstock or copy paper (one per student). Make a sample in advance to show the children. Read through the scripture reference, preferably at least twice to be thoroughly familiar with it.

Pray for spiritual insight, and for the children to have spirits that are open and receptive to the Word. Make copies of the note to parents (**figure 44**)

Welcome:

- ❖ The lure

Music: "Rise and Shine," Cedarmont Kids CD or DVD, "Who Built the Ark?," Cedarmont Kids

- ❖ The cast

Learning the memory verse before today's story should help reinforce the main ideas. Ask the children to repeat it after you, one phrase at a time until they can put it all together.

<u>Memory verse</u>: *There is a way that seems right to man, but in the end, it leads to death.* Proverbs 16:23

There is a way...
that seems right to man...
but in the end...
it leads to death. Proverbs 16:23

Because this lesson covers three chapters, it will be easier if you just read/tell the story, stopping every once in a while to have students find particular scriptures. Ask the children to find the <u>sixth</u> chapter of Genesis and leave their Bibles open to that page.

The Story of Noah:

Our story begins many, many years after God first created Adam and Eve. In fact, over 1500 years have gone by. Adam and Eve had two sons named Cain and

Abel. Years later, when Adam was 130 years old, they had another son named Seth, and after Seth was born, Adam lived another 800 years and had a lot of other sons and daughters! That meant that he was 930 years old when he finally died! Back then, people lived a lot longer than they do now.

Do you remember that Adam and Eve knew God personally? I imagine that they told their children about the God who had made them, don't you? And about the beautiful garden He put them in and how wonderful it was to be able to walk and talk with their Creator? It was theirs to enjoy...until the day that they disobeyed Him.

Who can remember what they did that made God sad and angry and caused them to be kicked out of the garden? Do you suppose that every day after that, when Adam had to go out into the heat and dig up the weeds and thorny bushes that he remembered why he was having to work so hard?

And, maybe, probably, their children told their children what their parents had told them. But over time, the truth about God kind of faded into the background, and after several centuries, (how many years in a century?) thousands of people were born and grew up to be adults who had never even heard of Adam and Eve and the serpent and the Garden of Eden.

Since many of them had never heard of the goodness of God, that they were to they became very wicked. They didn't love God nor live the way He wanted them to. How do you think God wanted them to treat each other? But they became very evil...they lied and stole things from each other, they cheated and beat each other up, and even killed each other. Men fought with other men, and women fought with other women, and men and women fought with each other. They were cruel. And, of course, their children mimicked their bad behavior. (Do you know what it means to mimic someone or some thing?)The Bible says that all their thoughts all day long were about the bad things they wanted to do.

The things that people did and thought and said made God very sad, and VERY angry! He was SORRY he had ever put people on the earth. He had made people to walk and talk and listen to and show kindness to each other and to be friends with him. But they weren't interested! They wanted to live their lives in whatever way they wanted, and what they wanted was to be mean to each other.

Well, God became so angry, that He decided He would just get rid of all of them...just wipe them off the face of the earth. Can you imagine how He felt?

But there was one man...only one man (and his family) on the whole earth who still knew about God and wanted to live like God wanted him to. Do you know his name? (Noah) Noah had a wife and three sons, Shem, Ham, and Japheth, who were also married. God decided to spare Noah's life and the lives of those in his family because he obeyed and honored God with his life. Let's look in our Bibles to find God's words to Noah.

(Ask the children to find verses 13 & 14 in Chapter six in their Bibles. Ask the children to read these verses.)

> *So God said to Noah, "I am going to put an end to all people, for the earth is filled with violence because of them. I am surely going to destroy both them and the earth. (v. 14) So make yourself an ark of cypress wood; make rooms in it and coat it with pitch (tar) inside and out.*

Then, God told Noah just exactly how big to build the ark. It was to be as long as one football field and ½ of another one...450 feet long and 75 feet wide and 45 feet high. (Compare the height and width with structures the children will be familiar with so they can get an idea about how large the ark would be. The average one story house is about 15 feet tall, roof and all, so the ark would have been about as tall as three houses stacked on top of each other.)
It was to have a roof on it, so the rain wouldn't get in and a door in its side and three decks for Noah and his family and all the animals that would ride in the ark.

Let's look at what God says in verse 17:
> *I am going to bring floodwaters on the earth to destroy all life under the heavens, every creature that has the breath of life in it. Everything on earth will perish.*

Then God promised He would take care of Noah and his family and bring them safely through the flood.

When Noah started building the ark, I imagine that the people who saw what he was doing must have thought he was crazy to build a boat out there on dry land, with no big lakes or rivers or oceans around to float the boat on. They probably laughed at him and made fun of him, but Noah believed that God would do exactly what He said He would do. So, Noah and his sons just kept on cutting down cypress trees and sawing them into planks of wood.

Back then, people didn't know anything about electricity or engines or motors. So, they didn't have any electric saws to cut the wood with or trucks to haul the lumber from one place to another. They may have used horses or donkeys to pull the trees they cut down to the site where they were building the ark. It took them a long, long time to cut enough lumber to build a boat as long and 1 ½ football fields and to make the three levels God had told Noah to make inside the ark and rooms for them to live in and probably stalls to keep the animals in.

They also had to gather enough food for all the animals to eat, and for themselves, too, because when the whole earth was covered with water, there would be no place to get more food.

Courtesy of Crisismagazine

Noah tried to warn the people that they needed to clean up their acts and start worshiping and obeying God before He destroyed them. Look at their faces. Did they believe him?

Image courtesy of Cagnz   Noah and his sons working on the ark...

Image courtesy of Freebible images

Image courtesy of Hiveminer... Noah and his family gathering food for themselves and the animals

When everything was prepared, God commanded Noah to take two of every animal, a male and female, that He considered unclean(the animals they were not allowed to eat), and seven of every clean animal (animals that it was OK to eat and that they could use for sacrifices to God) and also seven of every kind of bird. Why did he do this? Did he have to gather up the fish and sea creatures? Why not?

It would have been an incredibly hard job to gather up all those animals, even the creepy-crawlers, wouldn't it? So God helped Noah...He sent the animals to the ark, Himself! Cool, huh? Don't you think it made Noah smile when he looked up and saw all those animals strolling up to him and he realized how completely God was taking care of him?

117

Image courtesy of Biblicalfoundations

Then, when all the food had been stored away and all the animals had been put inside where they would be safe and dry and warm, God told Noah to get his family into the ark because things were fixing to happen! He was ready to send the flood.

Genesis, Chapter 7, verse 6 tells us that Noah was 600 years old when the floodwaters came on the earth. And, after Noah and his wife and his sons and their wives and all the animals were safely aboard the ark, verse 16 tells us that God, Himself, shut the door!
Then it came! The Bible tells us that three things happened to flood the earth. Do you remember when we were talking about how God created the earth that we learned that God separated the waters on the earth and the waters above the earth with a firmament that he called the sky? And we wondered what happened to the waters that were above the earth. We're about to find our answer.

Listen carefully…It would take a LOT of water to flood the earth so completely that even the tops of mountains could not be seen. So the Bible says in Chapter 7, verses 11 and 12, three things happened.
1. *All the underground springs burst forth…so all the water in the underground "rivers" rushed out and flowed over the earth…AND*
2. *The floodgates of heaven were opened. This was the water that had been above the sky…AND*
3. *The rain fell on the earth for forty days and forty nights.*

Image courtesy of Church of Jesus Christ

And all the people who had laughed at Noah and scoffed at God…died.

❖ The catch

Give each student a copy of the "boat" template. Ask them to turn the page over so the lines are on the other side. They need to choose a dark-colored crayon and color the backside of the boat <u>completely</u>. This is to make the boat waterproof. If they leave even a little "white" showing, that part will absorb water. Remember, Noah had to coat the inside and the outside of the ark with pitch (tar) so the wood wouldn't absorb the water and rot or make it so heavy it would sink.

When they've finished coloring the backside, they can cut out the boat and fold it upward along the lines. Use the plastic tape to seal the corners.

- ❖ <u>The feast</u>

Snack:

Figure 44 Note to parents

Today we learned about Noah and the great flood. We learned how seriously God regards disobedience and His judgment on those who disregard His laws and rebel against Him, as well as his mercy toward those who revere Him.

Today we learned about Noah and the great flood. We learned how seriously God regards disobedience and His judgment on those who disregard His laws and rebel against Him, as well as his mercy toward those who revere Him.

Today we learned about Noah and the great flood. We learned how seriously God regards disobedience and His judgment on those who disregard His laws and rebel against Him, as well as his mercy toward those who revere Him.

Today we learned about Noah and the great flood. We learned how seriously God regards disobedience and His judgment on those who disregard His laws and rebel against Him, as well as his mercy toward those who revere Him.

Today we learned about Noah and the great flood. We learned how seriously God regards disobedience and His judgment on those who disregard His laws and rebel against Him, as well as his mercy toward those who revere Him.

Today we learned about Noah and the great flood. We learned how seriously God regards disobedience and His judgment on those who disregard His laws and rebel against Him, as well as his mercy toward those who revere Him.

Today we learned about Noah and the great flood. We learned how seriously God regards disobedience and His judgment on those who disregard His laws and rebel against Him, as well as his mercy toward those who revere Him.

Figure 45

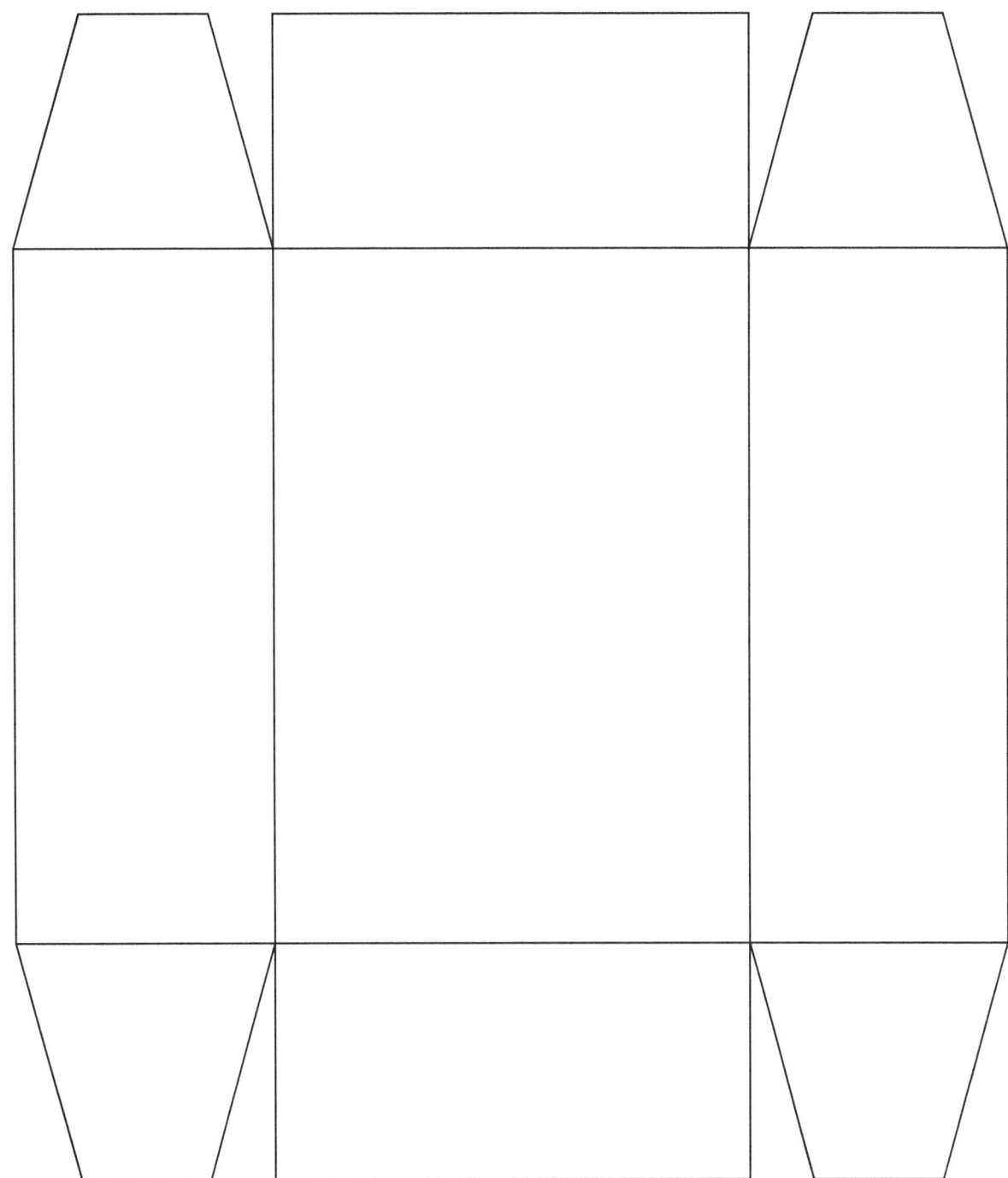

Ark template ©Deana Carmack

LET'S GO FISHING, LESSON 12
The Ark Lands on the Mountain

For your spirit:

> The little boy looked up at the woman who had just bought him shoes and a coat and a suit of warm clothes and asked, "Are you God?" She smiled down at him and replied, "No, son, I'm just one of His children." The little boy then said, "I knew you had to be some relation." *Dan Clark*
>
> To represent God to an alien world is often so difficult. We are all subject to times of self-absorption, depression, anxiety, etc. The only remedy for this that I know of is to ask the Holy Spirit to so infuse us that when people see our actions or hear our voices, it is Him they see and His voice they hear.

Scripture reference: Genesis 7:21-8:22, 9:3-17

Memory verse: (This is a long one and doesn't necessarily need to be memorized. The children can just read it with you a couple of times.)

God said, *"As long as the earth endures,*
  seedtime and harvest,
  cold and heat,
  summer and winter,
  day and night
  will never cease" Genesis 8:22

Emphasis: God promised that never again would he destroy everything on the earth.

Supplies needed:
- Bible for each child
- Music: "Rise and Shine" and "Who Built the Ark"…both by Cedarmont Kids
- Tempera paints…red, orange, yellow, green, blue, and violet
- Cotton swabs (Q –tips)
- Cotton balls
- Small Styrofoam bowls
- Glue
- A copy of the note to parents (figure 46) for each child
- A copy of the rainbow craft page (figure 47) for each child
- Snacks

Teacher prep: Read this historical account of what happened after the flood several times so you can answer any questions the children have. (When, occasionally, they ask us questions that we simply don't have the the answers to, we can only answer honestly that we don't know, but we'll try to find out. You might want to explain that there are some things that only God knows.) Make copies of **figure 46**, one for each student on either copy paper or white card stock. Make copies of the parent note. It's helpful if you "paint" a rainbow ahead of time following the instructions below for the children to see. Get out paints, cotton swabs, Styrofoam bowls ahead of time.

Welcome:

❖ The lure

Music: "Rise and Shine" and "Who Built the Ark"…both by Cedarmont Kids

❖ The cast

Pass out the Bibles and review the previous lesson:
    Preface it by saying something like: *Last week we learned about the time several thousand years ago when God destroyed almost every living animal on the earth.*
    Who remembers why He did that? (The people were so wicked.)
    How did he destroy the earth? Did it explode, freeze, burn up? (a flood)
    Did He destroy everyone? (no)
    Whom did he save? (Noah and his family)
    Why did God decide to save Noah and his family? (They loved God and lived the way He wanted them to.)
    Did God kill all the animals in the flood? (no)
    How many of each animal did God send into the ark? (2 of each unclean animal and 7 of each clean animal)
    He flooded the earth in three different ways. Do you remember what they were? (underground springs, rain from the sky, floodgates of the heavens)
    Let's see if we can remember last week's memory verse:
There is a way that seems right to man, but in the end, it leads to death.
Proverbs 16:23

Very good! Does anyone remember how long it rained? **(40 days and 40 nights)** *Okay, but as you know, sometimes after a big heavy rain or several days of rain, the ground doesn't get dry in just a few hours. Imagine how long it would take for all the rain to disappear after it rained so much that even the tallest mountain peaks were 20 feet under water.*

Let's see if we can find out exactly how long Noah and his friends had to stay on that ark. Let's open our Bibles and find the book of <u>Genesis</u> and turn to <u>Chapter 7</u>. Look at the very last verse <u>(#24)</u> of Chapter 7.

> The waters flooded the earth for a hundred and fifty days.

When we remember that most months have about 30 days in them, we realize that means that water completely covered the whole earth for about five months. Let's look back a few verses and see when the flood started. Look back in <u>Chapter 7 to verse 11</u>.

> In the six-hundredth year of Noah's life, on the <u>seventeenth day of the second month</u>, on that day (1) all the springs of the great deep burst forth, and (2) the floodgates of the heavens were opened. (3) and rain fell on the earth forty days and forty nights.

Forty days would be about a month and almost half of another month. So, at the end of forty days the rain stopped and the springs quit gushing forth, and the floodgates of the heavens were shut. That means that somewhere around the 10th of March, if we were using our calendar, God stopped the waters.

The recorded history of the very first calendars date back to the Neolithic age, 10,000-4500 B.C.) and were based on either the earth's orbit around the sun or on the moon's orbit around the earth. *But the months on their calendars didn't have the same names as ours do, and their years didn't start at the same time that ours do, but let's just call them by the names we know to help us understand a little better.*

What is the second month of our year? (February). So, when Noah was 600 years old, on the 17th day of a month we'll call February 17th, the flood started.

Skip down to <u>Chapter 8 and find verse 14</u>. Please put your finger on the verse when you've found it. What does it say?

> By the <u>twenty-seventh day</u> of the <u>second month</u> (in Noah's <u>601st year</u>...v. 13) the earth was completely dry.

Although the rain stopped, the whole earth was totally under water, and it took a long, long time for the rain to go down or to evaporate. On February 27th of the next year, when Noah was 601 years old, the earth was dry, and Noah and his family and all the animals could come out of the ark. That's one year and ten days that Noah and "the gang" were in the ark. That's like from your birthday in one year to your birthday the next year, plus ten more days. That's a long, long time to be stuck on board a boat with a whole lot of animals. But Noah probably didn't complain much because?...What happened to the people who weren't on the ark? Let's read the <u>21st and 22nd verses of Chapter 7</u>.

> Every living thing that moved on the earth perished (died)—birds, livestock, wild animals, all the creatures that swarm over the earth, and all mankind. Everything on dry land that had the breath of life in its nostrils died.

(If your students ask about whether or not fish survived, you can tell them that: *Most fish take in oxygen through their gills. **Gills** take **oxygen** out of the water. Fish force water through their **gills**, where it flows past lots of tiny blood vessels. **Oxygen** seeps through the walls of those vessels into the blood, and carbon dioxide seeps out. Fish may have nostrils, but they are for smelling. They don't take air through their noses like mammals do.*
 But there are some water animals that are mammals like land animals. Dolphins and whales are among them. These animals don't have noses to breathe through; instead they have holes on their backs that allow them to take in the oxygen. This is sort of a modified nostril...isn't God cool?...They can close these holes when they are underwater so they won't drown.
So, all sea creatures could have survived the flood.

Let's get on with our story. We have just read that the flood waters covered the earth completely for five months. Let's look again at <u>Chapter 8</u>, verses <u>1&2</u>.

> But God remembered Noah and all the wild animals and the livestock that were with him in the ark, and he sent a wind over the earth, and the waters receded.

How did God help the waters to dry up? (wind)
Now let's read verse 2:

> Now the springs of the deep (1) and the floodgates of the heavens had been closed (2), and the rain had stopped falling from the sky (3).

This verse says that the three events that happened to cause the flood had stopped, and God caused them to stop...kinda like turning off a faucet, right?

The water receded, that means to back away, steadily from the earth. On the 17th day of the seventh month, (that would be July on our calendar) the ark came to rest, landed, on the mountains of Ararat. But Noah and his family couldn't go out yet. They were on a mountain, but the land below the mountain, in the valleys and on the plains were still at least partially covered with water. Below is a picture of Mount Ararat, a mountain in a country that is now known as Turkey. It was close to other countries like Iran and Armenia.

[**Mount Ararat**, Turkish **Ağrı Dağı**, volcanic massif in extreme eastern Turkey, overlooking the point at which the frontiers of Turkey, Iran, and Armenia converge. Its northern and eastern slopes rise from the broad alluvial plain of the Aras River, about 3,300 feet (1,000 meters) above sea level; its southwestern slopes rise from a plain about 5,000 feet (1,500 meters) above sea level; and on the west a low pass separates it from a long range of other volcanic ridges extending westward toward the eastern Taurus ranges. The Ararat Massif is about 25 miles (40 km) in diameter.]

Yereman, Armenia, with Ararat in the background.

The waters continued to go down until the first day of the tenth month (our October. Remember that it had stopped raining in February) and tops of some of the mountains could be seen rising above the waters. But Noah and his family and the animals still couldn't leave the ark yet.

After 40 more days had passed, Noah opened a window in the ark and sent out a raven. Does anybody know what a raven is? (a blackbird) Why do you suppose he sent out a bird instead of one of the other animals? (Birds don't have to walk on land.) *The raven kept flying back and forth.*

Then he sent out a dove to see if the waters had gone down enough that the ground could be seen. But the dove could find no place to land, so it flew back to the ark.

Noah waited 7 more days and sent out the dove again. This time, when the dove returned, it carried a leaf from an olive tree! What did that mean? (The water had gone down enough that the leaves on the trees could be seen.) *So, Noah waited 7 more days and sent the dove out again. This time the dove didn't return. That's when Noah knew that the dove have found a place to build a nest. Yay!!!*

On the first day of the first month (January) Noah knew that the waters were gone from the surface of the earth. But it was probably still very muddy. But he could at least remove the covering from the ark so they could all see the sunshine and breathe some fresh air!

By the 27th day of the second month (February), the earth was completely dry. God told Noah to come out of the ark with his wife and sons and their wives and to bring out all the animals that went to "sea" with them.

Whew!!! What a long, long trip that had been. Don't you know they were all happy to be able to walk on solid, dry ground again?

Image courtesy of the Science photo library

When they had all left the ark, Noah built an altar (a table of stones) to the Lord and took some of the clean animals and clean birds and sacrificed them to the Lord. God had saved Noah and his family and the animals from an awful, awful death and had taken care of them the whole time they were on the ark. Noah was very, very grateful!

Image courtesy of Answers in Genesis

There was another big change...Do you remember what God told Adam and Eve they could eat in the garden? (fruit from the trees) And, later, when they had to leave the Garden of Eden, what could they eat? (grains and veggies, and other green plants that they had to grow themselves) Let's look at one more verse to find the change...<u>Chapter 9</u>, <u>verse 3</u>...

> *Everything that lives and moves will be food for you. Just as I gave you the green plants, I now give you everything.*

For the first time, God told them they could eat meat.
And then God made a covenant (agreement or promise) with Noah and his descendants and every creature that had survived the flood.
<u>Verses 12-16</u> tell us that He promised that never again would He destroy all life on earth with a flood. And He set His rainbow in the sky to remind them of that promise so that every time they saw a rainbow, they would remember God's promise, and He would remember it, too.

- ❖ The catch

Craft: the Rainbow: place small bowls or saucers on the table and pour small amounts of paint in each one (you'll need one bowl for each of the six colors. (Children may share the paints and the cotton swabs.) Place cotton swabs in each bowl of paint. The students can dab paint on the rainbow...beginning with the **top** color (red). The colors of the rainbow are, in order, red-orange-yellow-green-blue and purple...roy-g-bv. (We've omitted "indigo.") They "paint" the rainbow by making small dobs of paint. Encourage them to make dots close together instead of trying to use the swabs as paint burshes. Then they can glue the cotton balls at each end of their rainbows for the clouds.

- ❖ <u>The feast</u>

Snacks...

Figure 45 Note to parents

Dear parents: Today we learned about God's faithfulness in keeping Noah and his family and the animals safe from the flood for over a year. We also learned of His promise that He would never destroy all living things on the earth again.

Dear parents: Today we learned about God's faithfulness in keeping Noah and his family and the animals safe from the flood for over a year. We also learned of His promise that He would never destroy all living things on the earth again.

Dear parents: Today we learned about God's faithfulness in keeping Noah and his family and the animals safe from the flood for over a year. We also learned of His promise that He would never destroy all living things on the earth again.

Dear parents: Today we learned about God's faithfulness in keeping Noah and his family and the animals safe from the flood for over a year. We also learned of His promise that He would never destroy all living things on the earth again.

Dear parents: Today we learned about God's faithfulness in keeping Noah and his family and the animals safe from the flood for over a year. We also learned of His promise that He would never destroy all living things on the earth again.

Dear parents: Today we learned about God's faithfulness in keeping Noah and his family and the animals safe from the flood for over a year. We also learned of His promise that He would never destroy all living things on the earth again.

Dear parents: Today we learned about God's faithfulness in keeping Noah and his family and the animals safe from the flood for over a year. We also learned of His promise that He would never destroy all living things on the earth again.

Figure 46

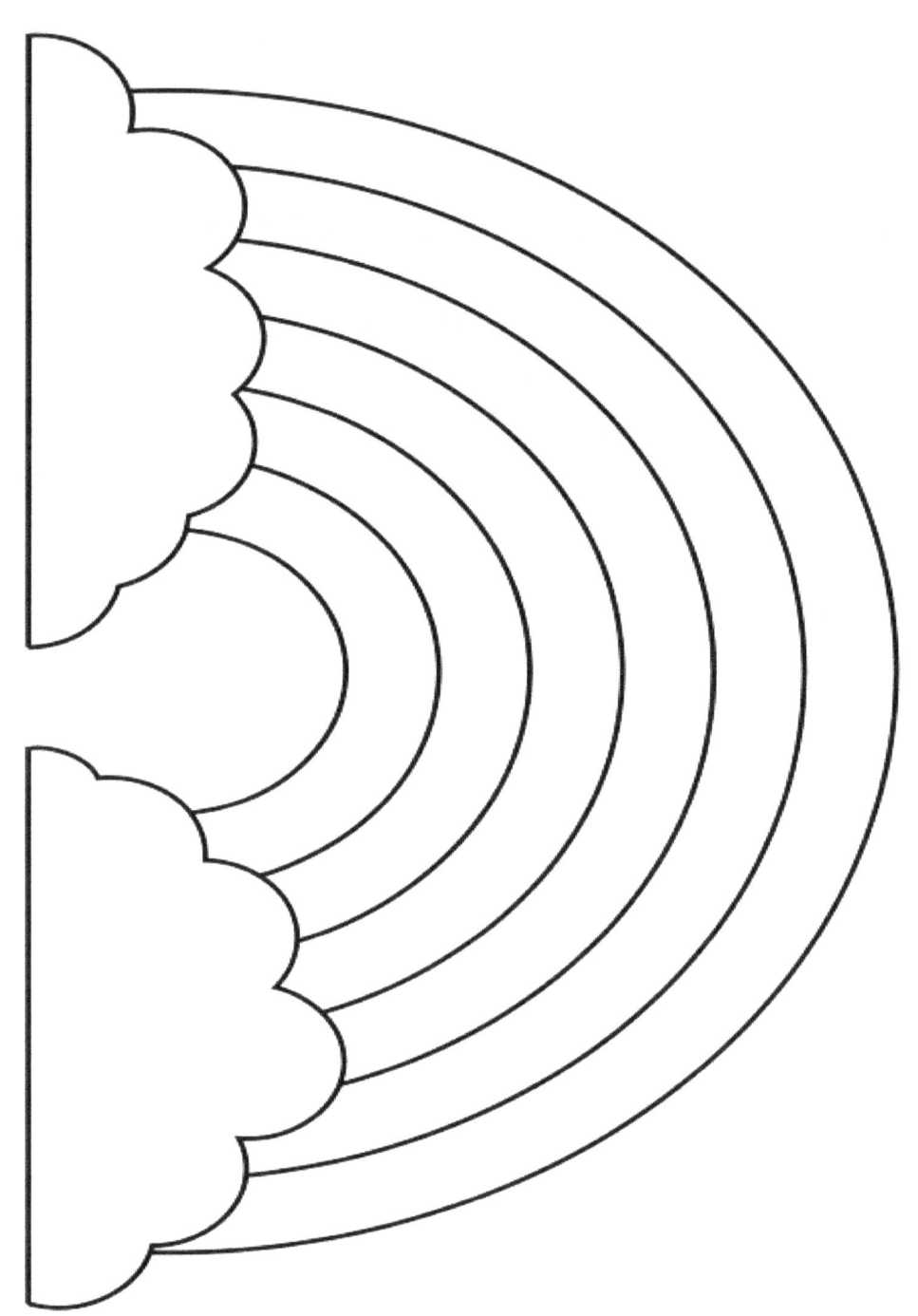

LET'S GO FISHING, LESSON 13
The Call to Abram

For your spirit:

> Do you know why you are teaching a Bible class for children? Is it because you were "roped" into it? Because no one else would do it? Because it is expected of you? Do you believe that this is your calling-- because you love the Lord and the children? The Bible clearly states that pastors and teachers are held to a higher standard. We must be willing to hold ourselves to this higher standard because others will be watching us. Our words should be kind and speak God's truth. We need to be dependable and punctual so the children we teach will know they can count on us. May God bless and guide you as you show, through your actions and the Word, who He is.

Scripture reference: Genesis 12:1-7, 15:1-6, 17:1-8, 18:1-15, 21:1-6

Memory verse: **_Abraham believed God, and it was credited to him as righteousness._**   James 2:23

Emphasis: God keeps His promises.

Supplies needed:
- Bible for each child
- One sheet (larger than 8 ½ X 11 inches) of black or very dark blue construction paper for each child (This will be the background for their stars.)
- A pencil for each child
- One sheet of white copy paper or card stock (Card stock will be less likely to warp.) for each child
- Tempera paints/watercolors/crayons in various light (pastel) colors (These are for the stars and will be glued to the black construction paper, so you'll need light colors.) You might want to use glitter paints.
- Glue (Elmer's, etc.)
- Scissors for each child

- Copies of the star patterns, several sets depending on the number of students you have. The kids can share these.
- Brushes for each student…wide, flats… (as opposed to "rounds")1/2 to 1" sizes (the larger he brush, the less time it will take)
- Water for clean up
- Paper towels
- Cover for table to protect it from paint spills and splatters
- Table or "clothesline" to place the painted papers on to dry
- Copies of note to parents, figure 47
- Globe of the world

Teacher prep: Pray for wisdom and guidance and insight as you prepare for this lesson. The object of all these lessons is to present God in such a way that the children believe He is who He says He is…that He is real…that He loves them…that He is faithful and all-powerful. Please read all the scriptures listed above. The lesson covers too much material for the children to read each verse, so you can let them read the verses listed below then tell them the rest of the account in your own words. You will probably want to have all craft materials ready and the star patterns cut out before class starts in the interest of time. You may also want to show the children a finished product of the craft, or you may choose to make one of your own as the children work on theirs.

Welcome:

❖ The catch

Craft: Give each child one sheet of white paper/card stock, pencil, scissors and pastel paints, including white.
Have them trace stars from the star patterns that you've cut out on <u>one side</u> of the paper/cardstock. (But don't have them cut the stars out yet.)

They will paint/color the other side. For watercolors children can use theirbrushes; for tempera, those who are brave enough can put large splotches of
paints on their papers and use their fingers to cover the paper. Warn them not to over-mix their colors, or they'll wind up with "mud".

When each child has finished, remove the papers, (or leave the papers where they are and move the children to another part of the room) so the papers can dry while you explore the lesson. Below are some samples of the colored side that may give the students an idea of what they're aiming for.

- ❖ The lure

Music: "Father Abraham" Cedarmont Kids

- ❖ The cast

Pass out the Bibles and ask the children to find Genesis in the Bible and turn the pages until they come to chapter 12.

Have any of you ever gone on a vacation? What did you have to do to get ready to go? What did you have to pack?
Have any of you ever packed up everything you owned and moved to another house or town or even to another country? What did you have to do to get ready? What are some things you needed to know about your journey before you left?
(how far it was, how long it would take, what kind of house you would be living in, etc.) *There's one very important thing you would want to know before you*

left…that is, where you were going, right? Because how would you know where to go if you didn't know where you were heading….?

Well, our story today took place a long, long time ago, and it's about a man named "Abram." Do you remember our story about Noah and the Ark? Well, Abram was Noah's great-great-great-great-great-great-great-great grandson. Hundreds of years and many generations had passed since the great flood.

Lots and lots, in fact thousands and thousands, of people had been born since Noah and the animals left the ark. And every one of them had descended from Noah and his wife and their sons and their wives. They built homes and cities all over the middle-eastern part of the world. (Showing where the Middle East is on the globe will prove helpful.) *In fact, one of Noah's sons, Japheth, wanted to be a seaman. He and his descendants built ships and sailed to other parts of the world.*

During that time the life spans of the people had become much shorter…they didn't live as long as they had back in Noah's day. Back then, most people lived 7-8-or even 9 hundred years or more. But by the time Abram came along, people were living one-or-two hundred years at the most.

Well, one day, God came to Abram, who was seventy-five years old and was living in a town called Ur. Isn't that a funny name for a town? How would you like to tell somebody that you lived in "Ur"?

Let's read the first three verses in Chapter 12.

> *(v.1)* **The Lord had said to Abram, "Leave your country, your people, and your father's household and go to the land I will show you.**

Listen to the amazing promise God made to Abram:

> *(v.2)* **I will make you into a great nation, and I will bless you; I will make your name great, and you will be a blessing.**

Here God has said that if Abram would do what He told him to, he would make him and his descendents into a great nation. Does anyone know what a nation is?

(a country) *He said He would make Abram's name great…that means that a lot of people would know who he was and that God was with him.*

(v. 3) I will bless those who bless you, and whoever curses you I will curse; and all peoples on earth will be blessed through you."

God is saying here that He would be good to the people who were good to Abram and cause bad things to happen to those who treated Abram badly. But the second half of that verse is the one that contains a really great promise. Let's look at that again, starting with "and all peoples." What does that say? It's very important. It says that "all peoples (that means everyone in the world) will be blessed through you."

Abram didn't have any idea what God was talking about. But, since we live several thousand years after Abram lived on the earth, we can know. Because Abram was the father of the Israelites, also called the Jews, and it was through his descendants that Jesus, the Savior of the world, would come.

Did you notice what God did not tell Abram? (where he was supposed to go.) *All God said was "go to a place that I will show you."*

Now, Abram was a wealthy man. He had lots of sheep and goats and cattle, and camels and donkeys, as well as servants, both men and women servants. So, he had to get everything together including household things, although they probably couldn't take much furniture because it would be hard to carry, and they might have nothing to live in but a tent.

But Abram trusted God and obeyed him. He gathered up all his belongings and left his father's home with his wife, Sarai, and his nephew named Lot.

The picture below shows what they might have looked like on their journey.

That was quite a project…they just set out, not knowing where they were heading but trusting God to show them the way. The Bible says they set out for the land of Canaan. (It was a town named after a man named Canaan, who was the son of Ham, and one of Noah's grandsons.)

When they got there, the Lord came to Abram and said, "To your offspring I will give this land." Does anyone know what "offspring" means? (children, grand-children, great-grandchildren, etc.)

The map on the next page shows how far Abraham traveled.

Many years passed, and Abram and Sarai traveled to many places, and all this while God still had not given Abram a son to carry on his name. How can you have lots of descendants when you don't have even one child?

One day, when Abram was 99 years old, that's 24 years after He first came to him and told him to leave Ur, God came to Abram again. This time it was to change his name. Let's find the 17th Chapter and read from there.

> (v.1) *When Abram was ninety-nine years old, the Lord appeared to him and said, "I am God Almighty/ walk before me and be blameless.* (v.2) *I will confirm my covenant between me and you, and will greatly increase your numbers."*

Do you remember what a covenant is? (a contract or agreement)

> *(v.3) Abram fell facedown, and God said to him, (v.4) As for me, this is my covenant with you: You will be the father of many nations. (v.5) No longer will you be called Abram; (which means "exalted father") your name will be Abraham, for I have made you a father of many nations.*

Kind of interesting how God said that, isn't it? He said, "I <u>have made</u> you the father of many nations." That means that in God's plans, it had already happened in the future. I think that God looks at time like we might look at a road map. He sees the future as if it were today. And still, Abraham didn't have even one child.

In Chapter 15: verse 5, God had told Abram to
> *"look up at the heavens and count the stars—if indeed you can count them. Then he said to him, "So shall your offspring be. <u>And Abram believed the Lord, and he credited to him as righteousness</u>."*

And that's our memory verse for today: " Abraham believed God, and it was credited it to him as righteousness." James 2:23

Ask the children to repeat it after you several times, in phrases, until they are comfortable with it.

Righteousness means "right-being," "right-doing", and "right-living." So, Abram's trust in God pleased God greatly and made him righteous in God's eyes.

Verse 15 says that God changed Sarai's name, too. From now on, her name was to be Sarah.

Some time later, the Lord appeared to Abraham again while he was sitting at the entrance to his tent. Abraham looked up and saw three men coming toward him. Abraham welcomed them and he and Sarah and his servants prepared them a meal of beef and cottage cheese (curds and milk) and homemade bread. After the men had eaten, they asked Abraham where Sarah was. He told them she was in the tent. She was curious about what they were doing there, so she hid and listened and heard them say...

Chapter 18: verse 10…

> *Then the Lord (or he) said, I will surely return to you about this time next year, and Sarah your wife will have a son."*
> *(v.11) Now Sarah was listening at the entrance to the tent, which was behind him. (v.11) Abraham and Sarah were already old and well advanced in years, and Sarah was past the age of childbearing. (v.12) So Sarah laughed to herself as she thought, "After I am worn out and my master is old, will I now have this pleasure?"*

Then the Lord asked why Sarah had laughed. "Is anything too hard for the Lord?" She was embarrassed and afraid so she lied, saying, "I didn't laugh." But the Lord said, "Yes you did."

And sure, enough, just like the Lord had said, almost a year later, Sarah had a baby boy. Abraham was 100 years old, and Sarah was about 90.

What does this story teach us about God? (that He is all powerful, that He can do anything, that we can trust Him because He always keeps His promises.)

Have the children cut out the star shapes they've drawn on the white side of their painted papers and glue them, colored side up to the black construction paper, representing the stars in the sky. (If the paints are not quite dry, they can gently blot them with paper towels.)

- <u>The feast</u>

Figure 48: Note to parents:

Today we learned about Abraham, who became the father of the Israelite nation. The emphasis was on how God is able to do anything and that He keeps His promises.

Today we learned about Abraham, who became the father of the Israelite nation. The emphasis was on how God is able to do anything and that He keeps His promises.

Today we learned about Abraham, who became the father of the Israelite nation. The emphasis was on how God is able to do anything and that He keeps His promises.

Today we learned about Abraham, who became the father of the Israelite nation. The emphasis was on how God is able to do anything and that He keeps His promises.

Today we learned about Abraham, who became the father of the Israelite nation. The emphasis was on how God is able to do anything and that He keeps His promises.

Today we learned about Abraham, who became the father of the Israelite nation. The emphasis was on how God is able to do anything and that He keeps His promises.

Today we learned about Abraham, who became the father of the Israelite nation. The emphasis was on how God is able to do anything and that He keeps His promises.

The catch

Star craft

144

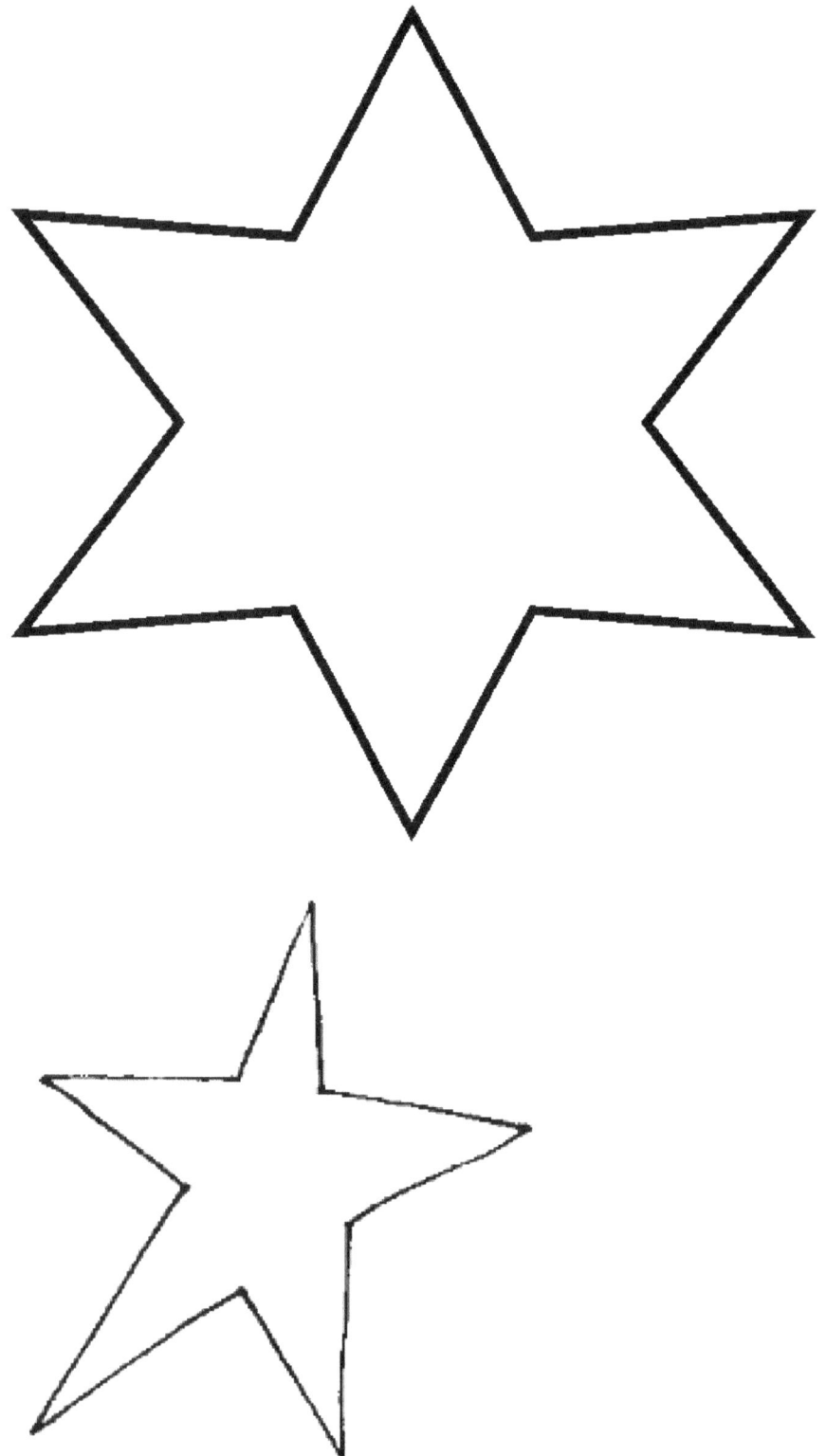

MEMORY VERSES

God is spirit, and his worshipers must worship in spirit and in truth. John 4:24

In the beginning, God created the heavens and the earth. Genesis 1:1

The heavens declare the glory of God. Psalm 19:1

For nothing is impossible with God. Luke 1:37

The word of God is living and active and sharper than any two-edged sword. Hebrews 4:12 (English Standard Version)

In the beginning was the Word, and the Word was WITH God, and the Word WAS God. John 1:1

Blessed are those who hear the word of God and obey it. Luke 11:28

God is light, and in him is no darkness at all. 1 John 1:5

For the wages of sin is death, but the gift of God is eternal life in Christ Jesus our Lord. Romans 6:23

There is a way that seems right to man, but in the end, it leads to death. Proverbs 16:23

Abraham believed God, and it was credited to him as righteousness. James 2:23

www.ingramcontent.com/pod-product-compliance
Lightning Source LLC
Chambersburg PA
CBHW081113080526
44587CB00021B/3581